KT-116-574

the
ILLUSTRATED BOOK of
QUESTIONS
and
ANSWERS

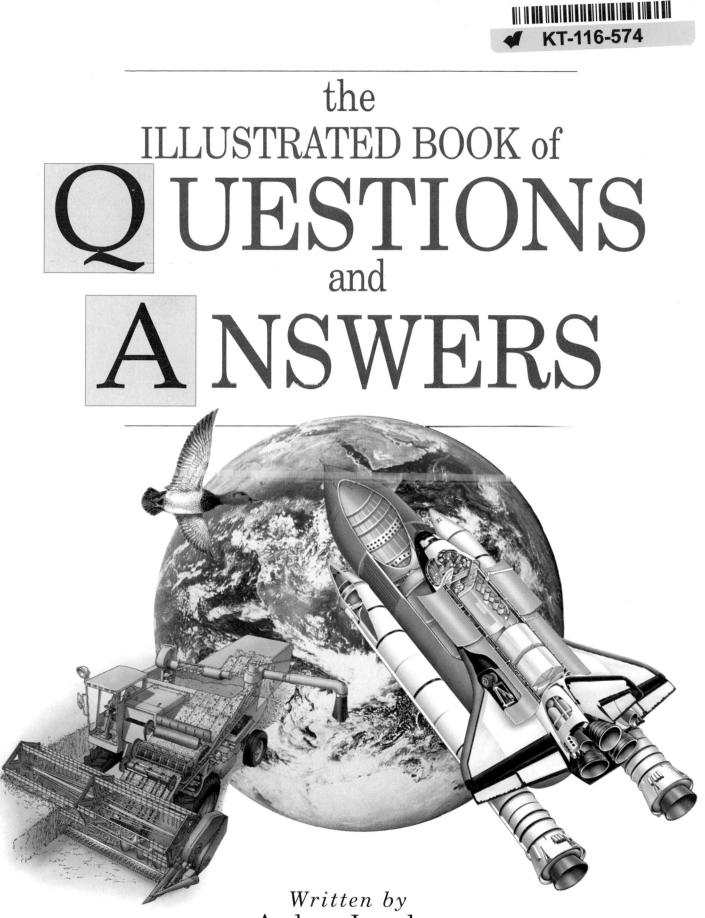

Written by
Andrew Langley

KIBWORTH
—BOOKS—

Published in 1993 by
Kibworth Books
Imperial Road
Kibworth Beauchamp
Leicester LE8 0HR
England

Copyright © Andromeda Oxford Limited 1993

Planned and produced by
Andromeda Oxford Limited
11-15 The Vineyard
Abingdon
Oxon OX14 3PX

All rights reserved. No part of this publication may be reproduced or
utilized in any form or by any means, electronic or mechanical, including
photocopying, recording, or by an information storage and retrieval
system, without permission in writing from the copyright holder.

ISBN 0 7239 0017 5

Printed in Spain by Fournier A. Gráficas, S.A. Vitoria

Photo Credits
Title page (Earth from space): NASA/Science Photo Library; p. 4
(Horsehead Nebula): Royal Observatory, Edinburgh; p. 5 (Milky Way):
Science Photo Library/Mt Palomar Observatory; p. 9 (moonwalk): NASA;
p. 17 (lightning): Jerome Yeats/Science Photo Library; p. 58 (buckle):
British Museum, (coin): Hirmer Fotoarchiv, Munich; p. 60 (gold clasps):
British Museum, London; p. 62 (statue): Museum of Mankind, British
Museum, London/Michael Holford; p. 70 (Hitler, Archduke Franz
Ferdinand): Hulton-Deutsch Collection; p. 87 (car): Hank Morgan/Sscience
Photo Library.

CONTENTS

Q How did the Sun and planets form?

A Nobody knows for certain. Most scientists think that the Sun, Earth and other planets (the Solar System) were formed from a mass of dust and gas. Nearly 5,000 million years ago, this mass started to shrink, and then spin and flatten into a disc. The centre of the disc became the Sun. The rest of the material turned into the planets (below).

Q What is a meteor?

A A meteor is a sudden streak of light in the sky (above). It is caused by a piece of rock from outer space reaching the Earth's atmosphere. The friction causes it to burn up.

Q What is a nebula?

A A nebula is a cloud of dust and gas in space. Some of the clouds block out the light from the stars behind. These are called dark nebulae. One of the best-known is the Horsehead Nebula (right). Other dust clouds reflect the light from the stars and shine brightly. These are called bright nebulae.

Q What is a black hole?

A Sometimes – no-one knows why – stars collapse in on themselves. This increases their gravity (a force that pulls everything inwards). Nothing escapes – not even light. These very dense bodies are called black holes (below).

Q What is a galaxy?

A A galaxy (below) is a huge spinning mass of stars in outer space. There are millions of galaxies, each containing billions of stars as well as gas and dust. Our galaxy is called the Milky Way. It contains about 10,000 million stars.

Q How did the Universe begin?

A Many scientists believe that all the material of the Universe was once crammed together in one place. Then, about 15,000 million years ago, an explosion or 'Big Bang' occurred. The material of the Universe flew out in all directions, forming galaxies and other bodies, mainly gas and dust. The effects of this explosion are still continuing, causing the Universe to expand (right). The galaxies still seem to be rushing away from each other.

Galaxies

SPACE

SOLAR SYSTEM

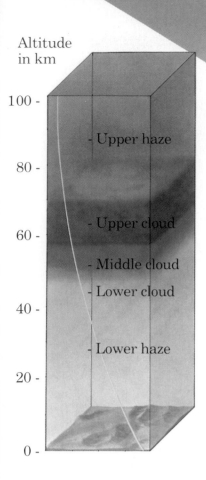

Altitude in km

- 100 — Upper haze
- 80 — Upper cloud
- 60 — Middle cloud
- Lower cloud
- 40 — Lower haze
- 20 —
- 0 —

Dish aerial

Cameras

UHF Aerial

Digging arm

Footpad

Q Which is the hottest planet?

A Venus. It is the second planet from the Sun. Venus is completely covered in dense clouds (left). These act like a giant greenhouse, raising temperatures to 462 °C. Several probes have landed on Venus but none has survived.

Q Is there life on Mars?

A In 1976 two Viking probes (above) landed on Mars and sent pictures of the rocky surface back to Earth. There were no astronauts aboard the Viking probes, so automatic soil samplers tested the red, dry soil for any sign of life. None was found.

Q Which planets have rings?

A Saturn, Jupiter, Uranus and Neptune have rings. The rings are actually tiny pieces of rock covered with ice. Rings may be fragments of moons which were destroyed, or they may have been part of the planets.

Q How many planets are there?

A There are nine known planets (below), but scientists believe that there is another planet millions of kilometres from the Sun. Scientists studying the outermost planets think they have found it, but nobody has yet proved that it exists. The biggest planet is Jupiter (143,000 km diameter), and the smallest is Pluto (2,000 km diameter).

Jupiter

Mercury

Venus

Earth

Mars

Sun

Q How hot is the Sun?

A The Sun is a vast ball of glowing gas (right). The temperature on the surface is 5,500 °C. At the heart of the Sun, temperatures are thought to be 15,000,000 °C! The heat is created in the core, or centre, by the nuclear fusion of hydrogen atoms. This is similar to the process that occurs in an exploding hydrogen bomb. Dark, cooler parts of the Sun are known as sunspots. Solar flares are great tongues of gas. All life on Earth is dependent upon the light and heat from the Sun.

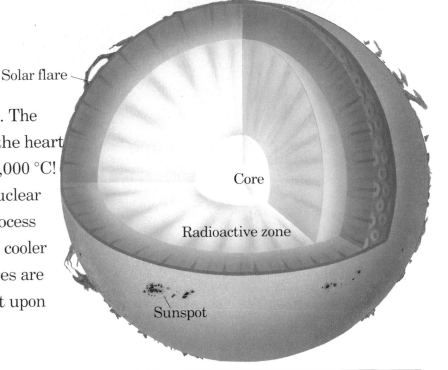

Solar flare

Core

Radioactive zone

Sunspot

Q How do we know so much about the planets?

A Space probes travel through the Solar System sending pictures back to Earth. One of the most important probes was Voyager 2, which was launched in 1978. It spent ten years in space, sending back valuable information.

TV Camera

Dish aerial

Thruster

Electronics compartment

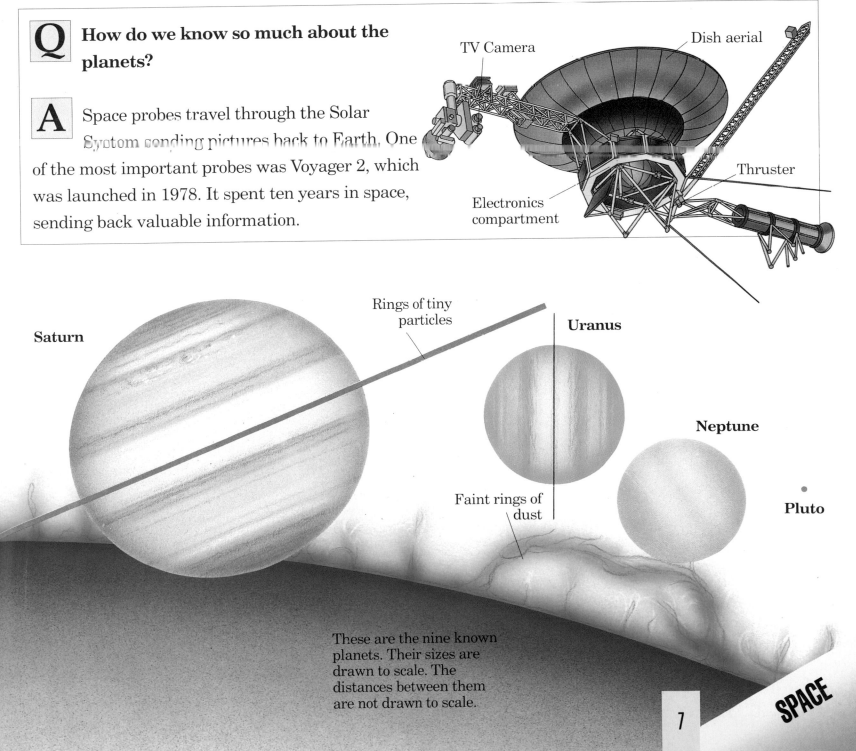

Saturn

Rings of tiny particles

Uranus

Neptune

Faint rings of dust

Pluto

These are the nine known planets. Their sizes are drawn to scale. The distances between them are not drawn to scale.

SPACE

Q **Why does the Moon seem to change shape?**

A The Moon shines because it reflects light from the Sun. However, as it travels around the Earth, we see more or less of its surface, making it appear to change in shape. The different shapes are called phases (below).

MOON

Q **What is inside the Moon?**

A No-one has ever examined the inside of the Moon (below). Its outside looks very different from the Earth, but inside it is probably the same. Beneath the thin outer crust is a mantle of solid rock. Under this is a thinner layer of molten rock, and at the centre is the core, about 1,420 kilometres from the surface.

First Quarter

Sunlight

Earth

New Moon

Full Moon

Sunlight

Last Quarter

70 km

1,000 km

350 km

300 km

Core
Molten
Rock

Mantle

Crust

Q **When did people first land on the Moon?**

A The Apollo 11 spacecraft (right) took off in July 1969. It was carried by a huge Saturn rocket for the first stage of its journey. Shooting out of Earth's orbit, Apollo travelled to the Moon. The lunar module separated and landed on the Moon's surface. Two of the crew, Neil Armstrong and Edwin Aldrin, became the first people to walk on the Moon.

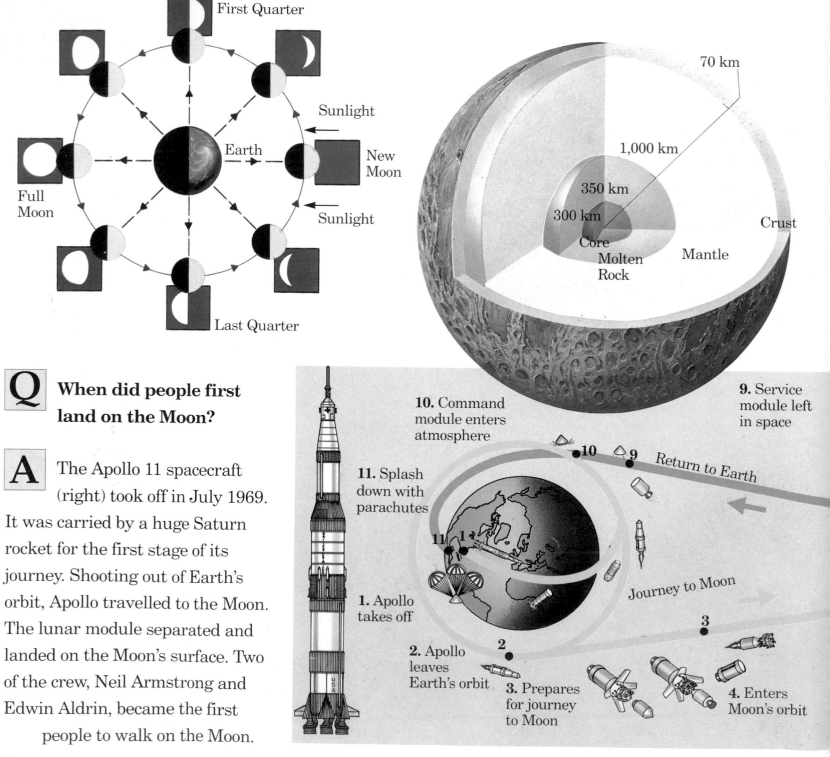

9. Service module left in space

10. Command module enters atmosphere

11. Splash down with parachutes

Return to Earth

1. Apollo takes off

2. Apollo leaves Earth's orbit

3. Prepares for journey to Moon

Journey to Moon

4. Enters Moon's orbit

SPACE

What is on the surface of the Moon?

A The Moon's surface (right) is covered with dust and rocks which have been smashed to pieces by showers of rock-like objects called meteorites. There is no water on the Moon. The Moon is pitted with craters, also caused by meteorites. Most are just tiny dents, but some are hundreds of kilometres wide. Some areas of the Moon look dark. People once thought these areas were seas. They were formed when meteorites cracked the Moon's surface. Molten rock bubbled up from below and grew hard. There are also many high mountains and deep valleys.

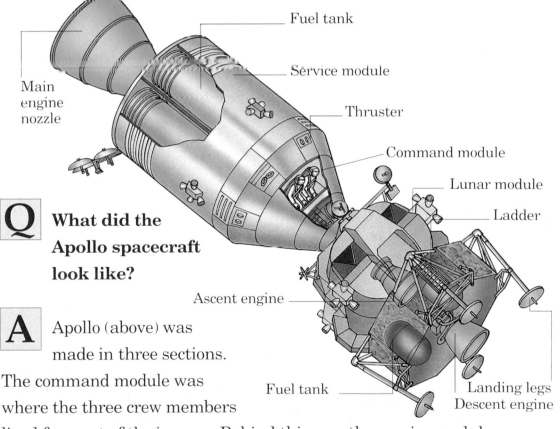

Fuel tank

Service module

Thruster

Command module

Lunar module

Ladder

Main engine nozzle

Ascent engine

Fuel tank

Landing legs
Descent engine

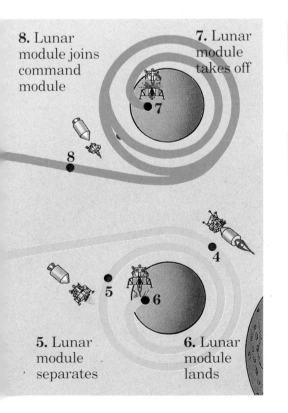

8. Lunar module joins command module

7. Lunar module takes off

5. Lunar module separates

6. Lunar module lands

Q **What did the Apollo spacecraft look like?**

A Apollo (above) was made in three sections. The command module was where the three crew members lived for most of the journey. Behind this was the service module. This contained the rocket engine and tanks for fuel and oxygen. The lunar module was used for landing on the Moon. It had four legs which spread out to support it on the Moon's surface. The lunar module and service module were left behind in space. Only the command module returned to splash down in the Pacific Ocean.

SPACE

EXPLORING SPACE

Altitude in kilometres

- 200
- 180
- 160
- 140
- 120
- 100
- 80
- 60
- 40
- 20
- 0

Q Where does space begin?

A The Earth is surrounded by a blanket of gases called the atmosphere, or air (left). These gases are thickest near the ground. The higher you go, the thinner and colder the air becomes. About 200 kilometres above the Earth, the air fades out altogether. This is where space begins, and where a spacecraft can start to orbit the Earth.

Dish aerial

Cosmic-ray telescope

Thruster

Q How do we try to contact other worlds?

A The methods used include beaming radio signals into deep space and sending messages on space probes. Pioneer 10 (left), which left the Solar System in 1983, carries a plaque showing Earth's position in relation to the Sun and information about the humans who built it.

Solar panel

Q What was the purpose of Skylab?

A This 'sky laboratory' (right) was sent into orbit around the Earth in 1973. The crew travelled to Skylab in an Apollo spacecraft. They crawled in through the docking hatch and passed the stores and oxygen tanks to get to the orbital workshop. Here, they carried out experiments and observed the planets and the Sun. At the other end of Skylab were the living quarters. One crew lived and worked in Skylab for 84 days. On top of Skylab were four solar panels which made power from sunlight.

Docking hatch

Oxygen tank

Q What is a space telescope?

A Earth telescopes have to look into space through the dust and moisture of the atmosphere. Telescopes out in space have a much clearer view. The Hubble Telescope (below) orbits the Earth.

Secondary mirror

Primary mirror

Guidance sensor

Solar panel

Q Which was the first space station?

A Salyut 1 (below) was the first ever space station. It was launched into orbit by the Russians in 1971. The crew was brought to Salyut I by a Soyuz spacecraft. Salyut's first crew spent 24 days on board – a record at the time.

Soyuz ferry

Docking port

Docking probe

Solar panel

Cameras

Working area

Thruster

Waste tank

Meteoroid shield

Water tank

Living quarters

Orbital workshop

Q How can we reach distant worlds?

A Ordinary rockets cannot travel far into outer space and back. In future, spacecraft may have engines which use nuclear power. Huge nuclear cruise ships (below) may be able to visit plancts in other solar systems.

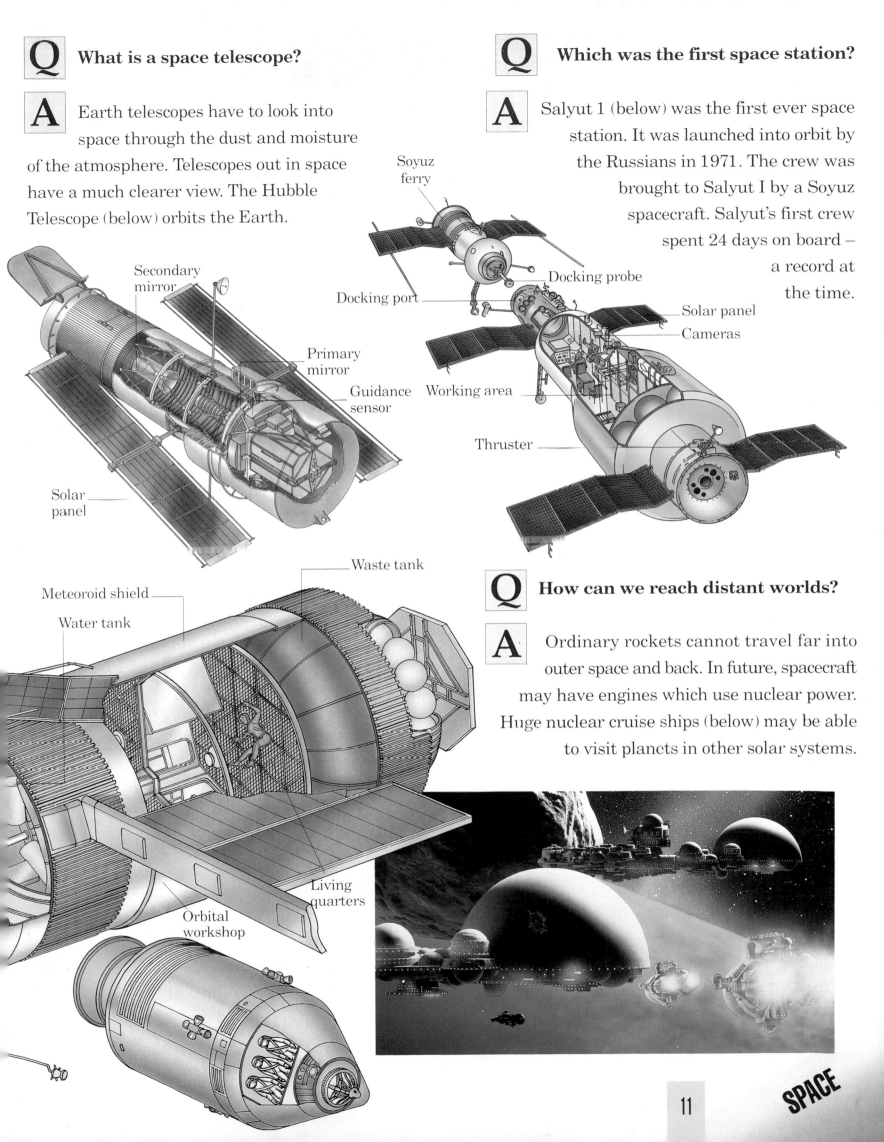

SPACE TRAVEL

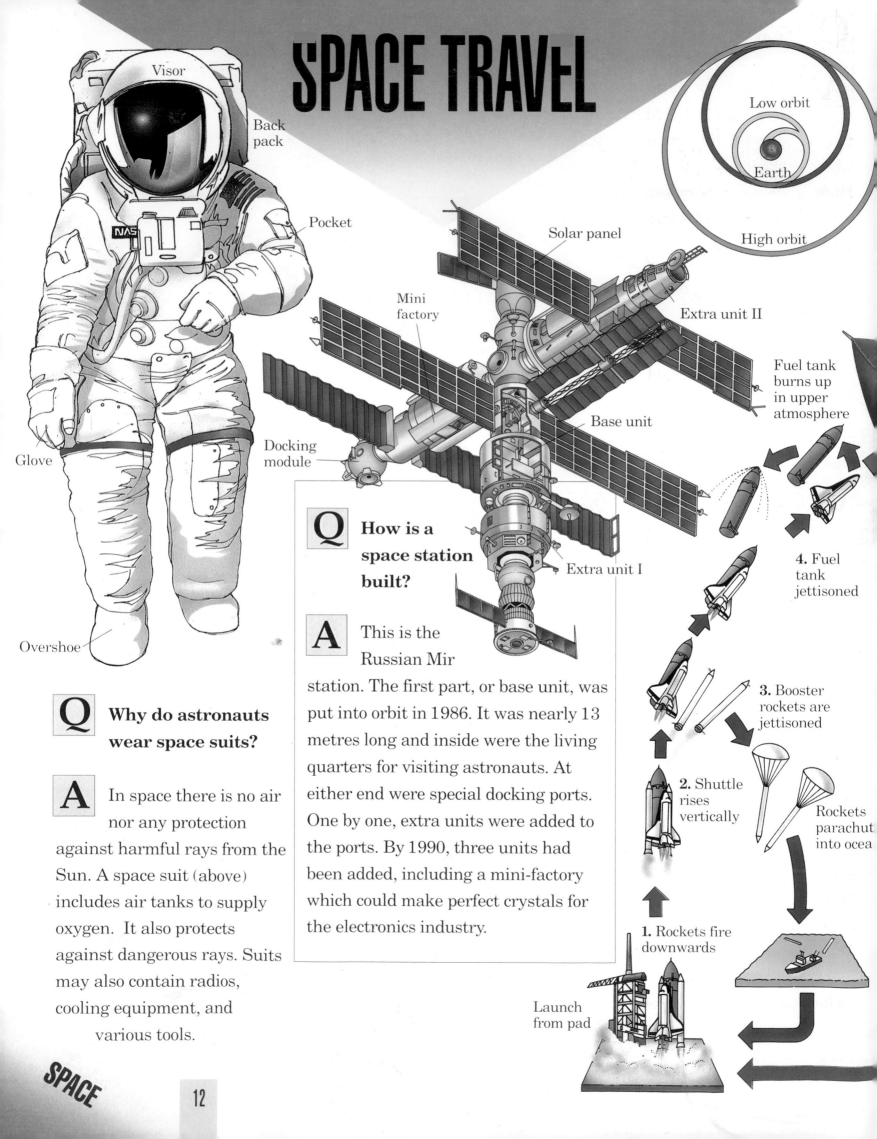

Visor

Back pack

Pocket

Solar panel

Mini factory

Low orbit

Earth

High orbit

NASA

Extra unit II

Base unit

Fuel tank burns up in upper atmosphere

Docking module

Glove

Extra unit I

4. Fuel tank jettisoned

Overshoe

Q How is a space station built?

A This is the Russian Mir station. The first part, or base unit, was put into orbit in 1986. It was nearly 13 metres long and inside were the living quarters for visiting astronauts. At either end were special docking ports. One by one, extra units were added to the ports. By 1990, three units had been added, including a mini-factory which could make perfect crystals for the electronics industry.

3. Booster rockets are jettisoned

2. Shuttle rises vertically

Rockets parachut into ocea

Q Why do astronauts wear space suits?

A In space there is no air nor any protection against harmful rays from the Sun. A space suit (above) includes air tanks to supply oxygen. It also protects against dangerous rays. Suits may also contain radios, cooling equipment, and various tools.

1. Rockets fire downwards

Launch from pad

Q What is an orbit?

A An orbit is the path an object takes around a star, planet or the Moon. Satellites circle the Earth in several different orbits (left). Those which take photographs use low orbits. High orbits are used by satellites which transmit signals such as television broadcasts.

5. Shuttle prepares for re-entry

Q How is the shuttle different from most spacecraft?

A Most spacecraft fly only once and their rockets burn up in flight. The space shuttle (below) is unusual because the craft and booster rockets can be used again. This means scientists can spend money on equipment which would have been too expensive to use only once. Satellites and other equipment are stored in the payload bay for use in orbit. Orbiting satellites can be put into the payload bay and brought back to Earth for repair.

6. Shuttle glows red-hot as it enters atmosphere

7. Shuttle tilts nose-down to glide

8. Pilot steers shuttle towards landing ground

Fuel tank

Electronic arm

Payload bay

Q How do spacecraft get into space?

A To enter space, rockets must escape Earth's gravity. This requires a speed of 28,000 km/h. Such speeds are easiest to reach by vertical take-off. But it takes huge amounts of power to lift a spacecraft. The space shuttle has a big fuel tank and two booster rockets to supply this power.

Main thrust engine

Booster rocket

Small engine for manoeuvring in space

9. Wheels are lowered ready to land

11. Shuttle returned to launch pad by plane

10. Landing on runway

PLANET EARTH

Q **What is inside the Earth?**

A The thin outer layer of the Earth (below) is called the crust. Beneath this is the solid mantle which makes up most of the Earth. The mantle is a mixture of rocks and minerals. Right at the centre of the Earth is the core of molten iron and nickel. The inner part of the core may be as hot as 9,000 °C.

Q **How were the continents formed?**

A Scientists believe that the continents (below) were formed from one giant land mass they call Pangaea. This broke in two, then split up into smaller land masses. These drifted apart until they reached their present places. But they are still moving!

286–248 million years ago

213–144 million years ago

65–25 million years ago

640 km

2,300 km

Lower mantle

1,800 km

Outer core

1,600 km

Inner core

Upper mantle

Crust

Q Why do we have seasons?

A The Earth takes one year to move round the Sun. But the Earth is tilted on its axis. This means that different parts of the Earth receive different amounts of sunlight, and so become warmer or colder as the Earth travels on its journey. When the North Pole is nearest to the Sun, the northern part of the Earth is warmest. Here it is summer. At the same time, the southern part is tilted away from the Sun, and is cooler. Here it is winter.

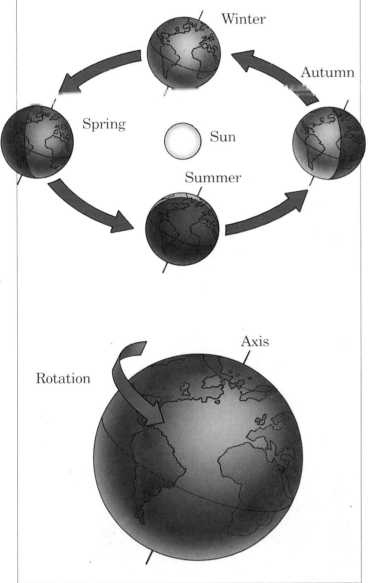

Winter

Autumn

Spring

Sun

Summer

Axis

Rotation

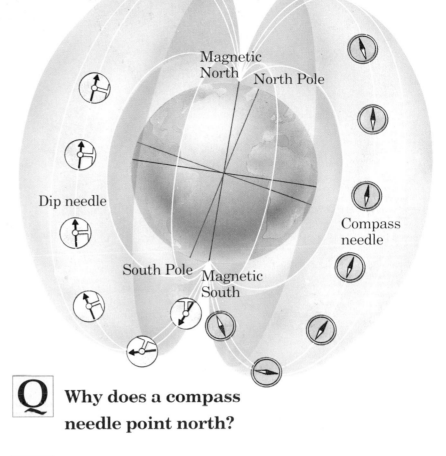

Magnetic North

North Pole

Dip needle

Compass needle

South Pole

Magnetic South

Q Why does a compass needle point north?

A The Earth is like a huge magnet with a force field which covers its whole surface (above). The poles of the magnet are near the North and South Poles. Magnetized objects – such as compass needles – are drawn to these poles. Therefore one end of a compass needle will always point north.

Q What were the ice ages?

A The ice ages (right) were periods in the Earth's history when the temperature became extremely cold. The last ice age ended about 10,000 years ago. Near the poles, a lot of water froze into ice. This meant that there was less water in the sea and the sea level dropped, leaving large areas of land uncovered.

Earth during ice age

Earth today

NATURAL FORCES

Gas, ash and rock fragments

Layers of lava and ash

Crater left by previous eruption

Lava

Q Why do volcanoes erupt?

A Volcanoes erupt when hot molten rock from inside the Earth forces its way through cracks in the Earth's surface (above left). This rock, called lava, flows from the volcano and cools.

Q What is a seismograph?

A A seismograph measures earthquakes. When an earthquake occurs, its hanging arm shakes, and the pen marks the paper on the revolving drum.

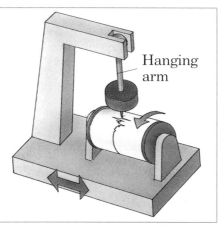

Hanging arm

Q What is a hurricane?

A A hurricane is a very strong whirling storm (right). The winds near the centre can reach 200 km/h. Hurricanes begin over warm tropical seas. The surface water heats up and evaporates to form clouds. This releases the heat and lowers the air pressure. Winds rush in from areas of higher pressure, swirling the clouds into a spiral. At the very centre of the hurricane is a calm area called the eye. As hurricanes move, they push the sea into huge waves and may cause floods. When the hurricane reaches land, it slowly grows weaker. But the high winds can still cause great damage to buildings and trees.

Q How do we measure wind speed?

A The speed of the wind is measured on the Beaufort Scale. This goes from 0 (calm) to 12 (hurricane). The scale describes how things behave at different wind speeds (right). At 1, light air, smoke drifts slowly. At Force 6, large trees sway, and at Force 10, buildings may be damaged.

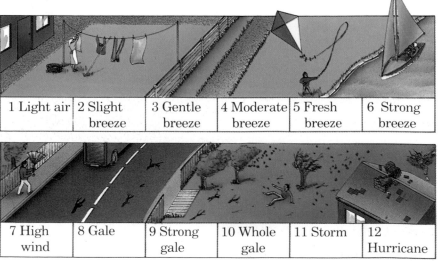

1 Light air	2 Slight breeze	3 Gentle breeze	4 Moderate breeze	5 Fresh breeze	6 Strong breeze
7 High wind	8 Gale	9 Strong gale	10 Whole gale	11 Storm	12 Hurricane

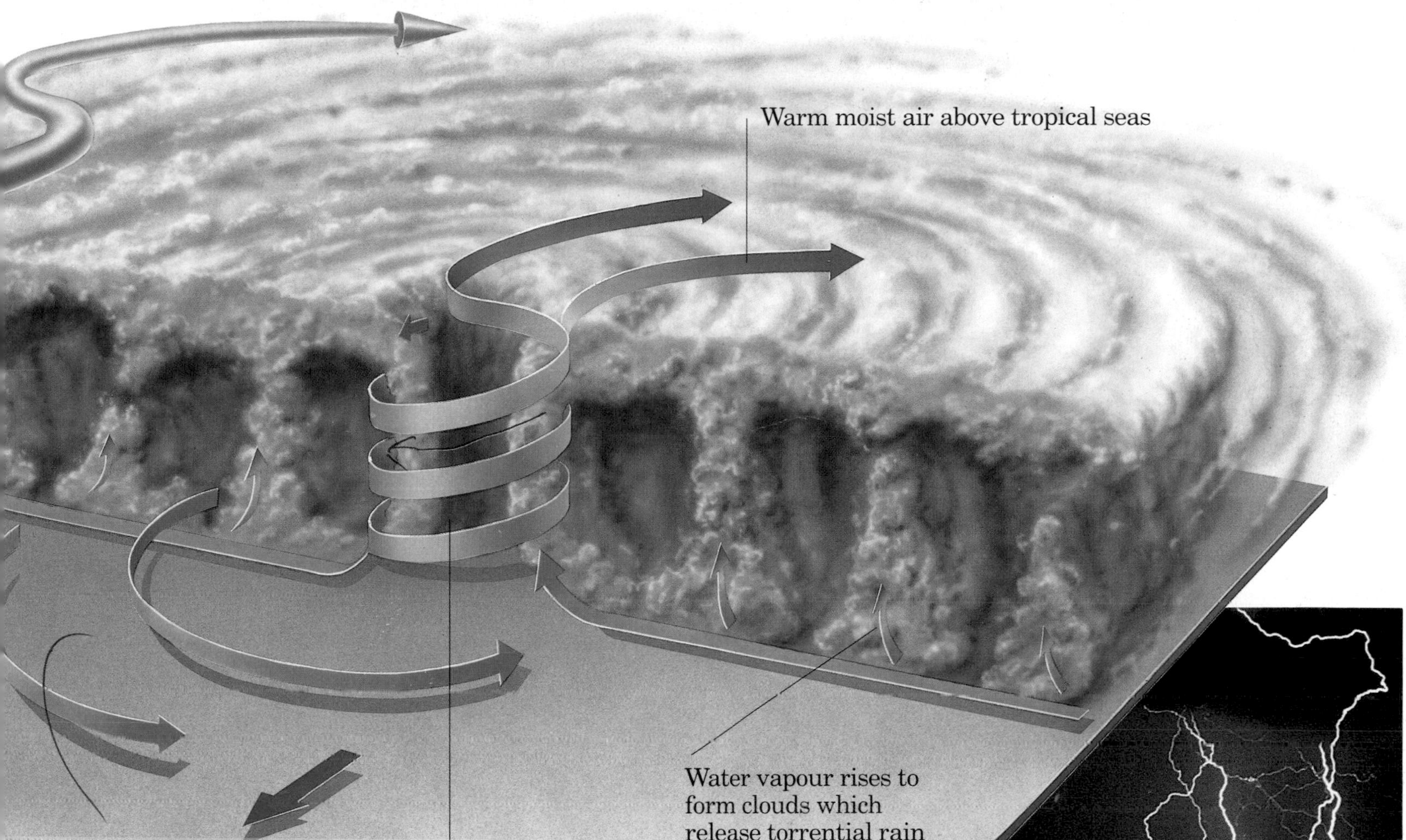

Warm moist air above tropical seas

Water vapour rises to
form clouds which
release torrential rain

Calm eye of the storm

Q **Where does the wind
come from?**

A When air becomes
warm, it rises.
Cool air is sucked in
to replace it, and
this movement of
air causes a wind.
The warm air
expands and cools
before falling to the
land again. This
constant movement of
air forms a regular pattern
of winds around the world (right).

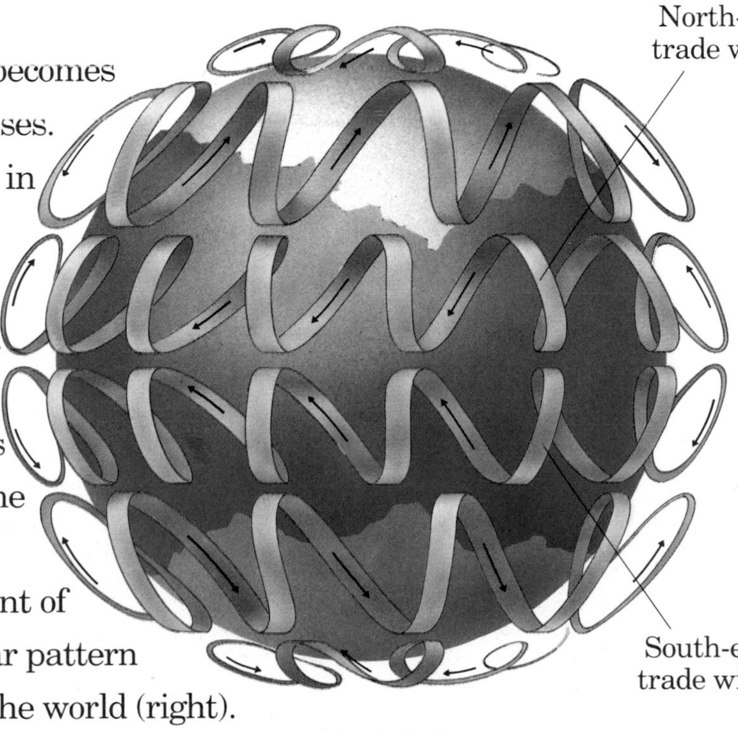

North Pole

North-east
trade winds

South-east
trade winds

South Pole

Q **What causes lightning?**

A Lightning is caused when
a large electric charge
builds up in a cloud as a result
of ice and water particles
rubbing together. The electric
charge flashes to Earth, or to
another cloud, as lightning
(above).

WATER

Q What lies under the oceans?

A The sea floor (below) has plains, valleys, mountains and even volcanoes. Near the shore is the shallow continental shelf. This slopes to the plain, about 4,000 metres below. On the plain are deep cracks called ocean trenches, and raised areas called ridges.

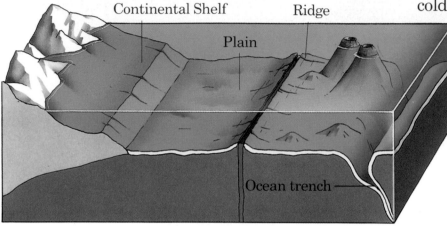

Continental Shelf   Ridge

Plain

Ocean trench

Q How much of the Earth is covered by oceans?

A The oceans cover 71 per cent of the Earth. The continents are actually huge islands in a continuous stretch of water (below). The water flows around the world in a pattern of warm and cold currents.

Q How does the sea change the coastline?

A The waves of the sea constantly pound the edge of the land (right). They change the shape of the coastline in two ways. First, the waves smash against the rocks and grind them into pebbles and sand. They hurl the pebbles at the cliffs, slowly wearing them away. But the sea also moves the sand and pebbles to other places. Beaches are formed and the coastline is built up where the sea drops them.

Waves wear away cliffs

Waves grind down pebbles to form sand

Q What is the water cycle?

A Water is always on the move (right), changing from liquid to vapour and back to liquid. The heat of the Sun evaporates water from the oceans, lakes and rivers. Plants also release moisture from their leaves. The moisture rises into the air and cools to form clouds. Winds blow the clouds towards the land. Here the clouds grow cooler, especially over high ground, and it starts to rain. The rain drains into rivers and lakes and then back into the sea.

Snow and rain

Evaporation from rivers and lakes

Evaporation from oceans

Rainfall over oceans

Evaporation from soil

Evaporation from vegetation

Q What is a glacier?

A A glacier (right) is a river of ice which forms in cold regions high up in the mountains or near the poles. It slides very slowly downhill, a few metres each year. It carries a mass of rocks which scrape away the valley walls and floor. It later deposits rocks and earth in huge ridges called moraines. If a glacier reaches the sea, large pieces break off and float away as icebergs.

Icefall

Arête, a narrow ridge left between glaciers

Avalanche

Moraine

19

OUR WORLD

LANDSCAPE

Q **How are mountains made?**

A The surface of the Earth consists of a series of huge plates. These move slowly about and sometimes collide with each other (above). When this happens, the edges of the plates are pushed up and the layers of rock crumple and fold. Over millions of years, the folds form chains of mountains.

Q **How are caves formed?**

A Many caves are found in limestone rock (below). They are formed when rainwater soaks down through cracks in the rock. The water dissolves the limestone, making the cracks bigger. Now streams can flow in underground. They wear away weak parts of the rock to make caves. Sometimes water drips into the caves. The dissolved limestone forms hanging spikes called stalactites. Pillars called stalagmites form on the floor below.

Q **What is soil made from?**

A Soil is a mixture of rock particles and humus, which is made from the tissues of dead plants and animals. The humus breaks down and releases minerals which help plants to grow. Below the soil is the rocky subsoil and beneath that the solid rock, known as bedrock.

Crack where rainwater has worn away rock

Stalactite

Rockfall   Stalagmite

Underground stream

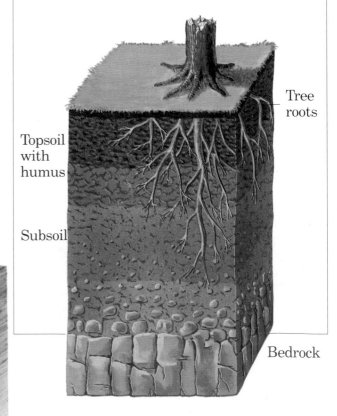

Tree roots

Topsoil with humus

Subsoil

Bedrock

Q How can a river alter the landscape?

A Rivers begin with water flowing downhill (left). Young mountain streams often originate in glaciers. The swiftly flowing water can carve away rock and produce deep V-shaped valleys. As it reaches the hills, it moves more slowly, producing broad valleys. When the river reaches flat plains, it may meander in wide curves. If a curve becomes cut off, it forms a lake. As a river reaches the sea, it deposits stones and sand to form a delta of low land along the coast.

Q What is an iceberg?

A An iceberg is a piece of ice from a glacier or polar ice sheet which breaks off at the coastline and then floats in the sea. Only one-eighth of an iceberg shows above the sea's surface. This is why they are dangerous to ships. Icebergs may drift for two years before melting.

Q What is a mineral?

A A mineral is any one of the non-living substances from which the Earth is made. There are about 3,000 different minerals. Some minerals combine to form rocks. Other minerals are rare and precious, such as gold, silver and diamonds. Minerals are used to make many things from the lead inside pencils to the mercury inside thermometers.

Granite   **Marble**

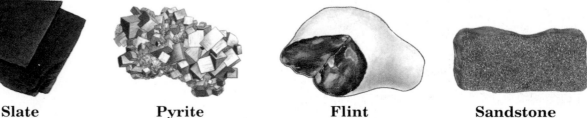

Limestone   **Slate**   **Pyrite**   **Flint**   **Sandstone**

21

HABITATS

Q What is succession?

A Succession is the natural process by which habitats change, and one community of plants and animals is slowly replaced by another. The picture below shows an example of succession at work as a temperate lake silts up, and the dry land eventually becomes oak woodland.

Beaver's lodge

Q Can animals alter a habitat?

A Some animals can change their habitats. Beavers cut down trees with their strong teeth. Then they use the trees, together with mud and stones, to dam streams. Their homes, called lodges, are large piles of sticks built up from the bottom of the ponds they have created (above). Here, they raise their young, safely away from predators.

50 years

20 years

10 years

After 5 years

Lake

Plankton

Shark

Dolphin

Bluefin tuna

Giant squid

Q What is a habitat?

A A habitat is a place where plants and animals live together as a community. Most creatures only live in one type of habitat, and cannot survive elsewhere. Look at the different habitats seen (right) in the picture of an ocean. Most life is found near the surface. A few species of fish and squid live in deeper water. The seabed is the realm of specially adapted marine creatures that cannot survive elsewhere in the ocean.

Deep-sea jellyfish

Skate

Angler fish

OUR WORLD

22

Q What are the world's
main land habitats?

A The world's land habitats
range from cold tundra and
mountains, through hot deserts and
grasslands, to the temperate woods
and tropical rainforests, teeming
with life. The ten major habitats are
shown below. Each has its own type
of climate, and plant and animal life.

Q How do wading birds avoid competing for food?

A These wading birds all have specially shaped beaks for
catching different creatures on the seashore. So they do
not compete for food although they live in the same habitat.

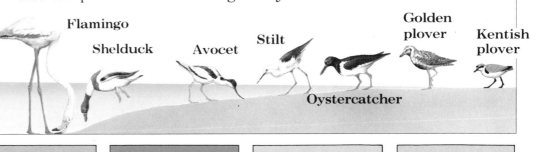

Flamingo · Shelduck · Avocet · Stilt · Golden plover · Kentish plover · Oystercatcher

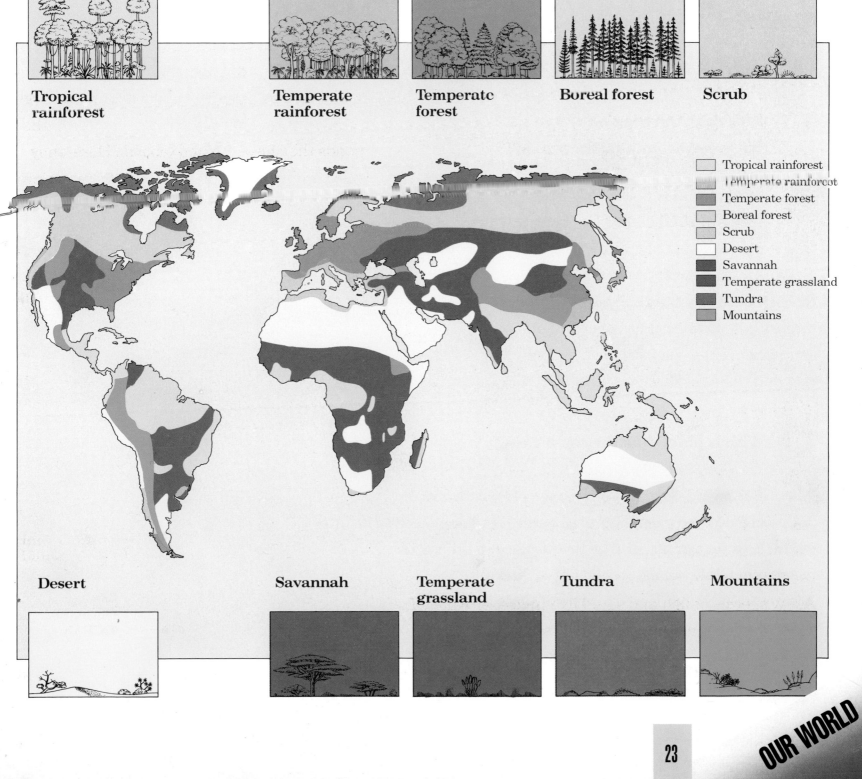

Tropical rainforest · **Temperate rainforest** · **Temperate forest** · **Boreal forest** · **Scrub**

Tropical rainforest
Temperate rainforest
Temperate forest
Boreal forest
Scrub
Desert
Savannah
Temperate grassland
Tundra
Mountains

Desert · **Savannah** · **Temperate grassland** · **Tundra** · **Mountains**

23

OUR WORLD

WORLD FACTS

 Q Which is the world's largest country?

 A Canada has an area of 9,976,000 square kilometres, making it the largest country in the world. Close behind are China, with 9,597,000 square kilometres, and the USA, with 9,363,000 square kilometres.

Q Where is the biggest freshwater lake in the world?

A A lake is a large area of water surrounded by land. The biggest freshwater lake is Lake Superior in North America, which stretches for 82,350 square kilometres. Some of the largest lakes are actually seas, full of salt water. These include the Caspian Sea and the Aral Sea.

Q Which place has the least rain?

A The world receives an average of 86 centimetres of rain, snow and hail each year. But some places get little or no rain at all. The driest place in the world is Arica in Chile, which receives less than one millimetre of rain a year. In parts of West Africa and South America, rain falls nearly every day.

 Q Which is the biggest island in the world?

A Greenland is by far the world's biggest island, at 2,175,600 square kilometres.

Greenland

Canada

NORTH
AMERICA

Lake
Superior

ATLANTIC
OCEAN

Sahara

PACIFIC
OCEAN

SOUTH
AMERICA

Arica

Chile

ANTARCTIC
OCEAN

OUR WORLD

24

Q Which is the world's smallest country?

 A Vatican City is the world's smallest country. It covers only 44 hectares and lies inside another city – Rome, in Italy. Yet it is an independent state, with its own bank, railway station, and postage stamps. It is the centre of the Roman Catholic Church.

 Q Which is the largest desert in the world?

A A desert is a hot, dry region where there is low rainfall and little can grow. By far the biggest desert region is the Sahara in North Africa. This covers over nine million square kilometres. About one-seventh of the world's land area is desert.

ARCTIC OCEAN

Aral Sea

ASIA

EUROPE

Vatican City

Caspian Sea

K2

China

Kanchenjunga

Mount Everest

AFRICA

INDIAN OCEAN

AUSTRALASIA

ANTARCTICA

Q Where is the world's highest mountain?

A The world's highest mountain is Mount Everest. It lies in the Himalayas range in Central Asia and rises 8,848 metres above sea level. Some of the highest mountains in the world lie in this range. In the same range are K2 (8,611 metres) and Kanchenjunga (8,598 metres).

 Q Where is the coldest place in the world?

A Antarctica is the coldest region in the world. It is the continent which surrounds the South Pole and is covered in a layer of ice about two kilometres thick. The temperature rarely rises above freezing point. In 1983, a temperature of -89.2 °C was recorded – the world's lowest ever.

OUR WORLD

Q How does a diver breathe under water?

A A diver uses scuba equipment to breathe underwater. Scuba stands for 'self-contained underwater breathing apparatus'. On his back, the diver (above) has metal tanks which hold a mixture of oxygen and other gases so that he can breathe. The gases reach his mouth through a hose.

Q What pre-flight checks must a pilot perform before take-off?

A The pilot has to check both inside and outside the plane before he takes off. In the cockpit (above), he checks that there is enough fuel for the flight and that all the engine and flight controls are working properly.

Q What do vets do?

A Vets only spend part of their time in the surgery (left). There, they treat family pets, such as rabbits, dogs and cats. The rest of the time, vets travel to see bigger animals, especially on farms. They care for cows, pigs, sheep and other livestock and help to prevent the outbreak of animal diseases. Some vets inspect meat and eggs, or test milk and other animal products.

Q How does a farmer prepare soil for crops?

A First, the farmer ploughs the land (right). The sharp ploughshares dig into the soil and turn it over. To break up the lumps of soil, the farmer pulls a sort of rake called a harrow, either with discs or with curved spikes, over the field. He may also crush the lumps with a heavy roller. At this stage, fertilizers are spread on the field to make the crops grow quickly. Then the field is ready for sowing.

Ploughshare

Q Which fish are caught by deep sea fishermen?

A Most fish are caught by modern fishing boats. Nearly 80 million tonnes of fish are caught every year. The main fish caught near the seabed are cod, flounder, hake and pollock. These are often caught in funnel-shaped trawl nets. Fish enter through the net's wide mouth and collect at the narrow tail end. The fish must be preserved quickly or else they will spoil. Most deep sea fishermen pack their catch in ice (below), or deep freeze it, before sailing home.

Q How much kit does a professional footballer use?

A A league football club has 20 to 30 full-time players. Each player has at least five pairs of boots, including training shoes and special boots for use on hard ground. The team also uses nearly 1,000 pieces of clothing. These include match strip and tracksuits.

OUR WORLD

Q Which were the first animals to fly?

A Insects have been able to fly for far longer than any other animal. Winged insects probably developed from types of worms which lived in the sea. Some insects were huge, like the giant dragonfly *Meganeura* (right), which lived about 300 million years ago. Its wingspan was more than 60 centimetres.

Q Why did animals begin to live on land?

A The very earliest creatures lived in water. Then plants began to grow on the land. These provided a new source of food and some animals left the water. They developed lungs, instead of gills, for breathing. Their fins developed into legs to help them move on land. The first to come on land were the amphibians such as *Ichthyostega*. They had fish-like heads and tails, but stronger backbones and stout legs.

Q Which was the earliest known bird?

A The *Archaeopteryx* (below) was a bird which lived about 150 million years ago. It looked like a small dinosaur but was covered with feathers. It also had wings which it spread for gliding through the air. Nobody knows for certain whether it could fly properly. Unlike today's birds, *Archaeopteryx* had three claws on each wing which it used for climbing trees. It also had teeth and a long tail covered with feathers.

Q Why do dinosaurs have such long names?

Corythosaurus

Tyrannosaurus

A The names of dinosaurs look confusing but they each describe something about their owner (right). The names are made up of Greek and Latin terms. The word dinosaur itself means 'terrible lizard'. *Corythosaurus* means 'helmeted reptile'. *Alamosaurus* means 'lizard from Alamo'. *Triceratops* means 'face with three horns'. *Tyrannosaurus* means 'tyrant reptile'. *Ornithomimus* means 'imitator of birds'. *Pachycephalosaurus* means 'reptile with a thick head'.

Alamosaurus

Triceratops

Ornithomimus

Pachycephalosaurus

Q What were early humans like?

A The first human beings (below) probably lived about 2 million years ago in East Africa. Their faces were ape-like and their bodies were covered with hair. They walked upright and used sticks, stones and bones as tools.

Q What is a fossil?

A A fossil is the remains of a plant or animal which lived millions of years ago. Some, like this insect (1), have been covered in a hard substance called amber. This is the sap from ancient pine trees. But most, like the plants (2, 3 and 5), have been turned into stone. The shell (4) is of an extinct marine animal called an ammonite.

NATURE

PLANTS

Q How do plants spread their seeds?

A Plants have many ways of spreading their seeds (right). Some seeds grow inside fruits. These are eaten by animals and emerge in their dung. Some plants have seed cases which 'explode' or split open, throwing seeds in all directions. Some seeds, such as nuts and grains, are gathered by animals and stored in larders. Others have tiny hooks which cling to the coats of passing animals. Dandelion and maple seeds are so light that they are blown by the wind.

SEEDS CARRIED BY THE WIND

Maple

Dandelion

SEED INSIDE FRUITS EATEN BY ANIMALS

Fig

Blackberry

Plum

SEEDS CARRIED BY ANIMALS

Hazelnut

Wheat   Carrot

SEED CASES WHICH SPLIT OPEN

Foxglove

Pea

Shepherd's purse

Q What are the different parts of a flower ?

A The parts of a flower are attached to a base, called a receptacle. The outer green parts are called sepals. Inside these are the petals. Inside the petals are the stamens and the carpels: male and female parts which produce new seeds.

Receptacle

Petal

Sepal

Carpel
(female)

Stamen
(male)

Q Why are flowers brightly coloured?

A Flowers (below) have brightly coloured petals which attract bees and other insects. The insects feed on the sugary liquid called nectar inside the flower. Grains of pollen stick to these insects. When the insect visits another flower some of this pollen sticks to the new flower and pollinates it.

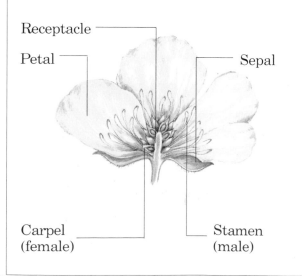

Lupin

Clarkia

Bougainvillea

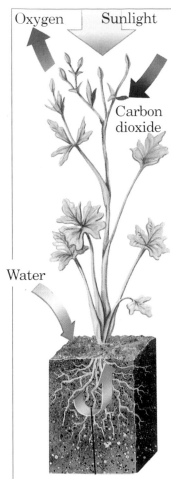

Oxygen Sunlight

Carbon dioxide

Water

Water and minerals

Q How do plants grow?

A Plants need three things to make them grow – sun, air and water. The leaves absorb sunlight and a gas called carbon dioxide from the air. The roots draw up water and minerals from the soil. Cells in the leaves use the energy from the sunlight to change the water and carbon dioxide into sugar. This is the plant's food. In turn, the plant breathes out oxygen into the air. This process is called photosynthesis.

Q How do plants survive in the desert?

A The soil of the desert is hard and dry. The air is very hot, and there is little rain. So desert plants have developed special ways of living in such a harsh place. Some, like the cactus (right), can store water in their fleshy leaves. The spikes help protect the plant from animals and also keep the leaves cool by casting tiny shadows.

Cedar of Lebanon

Red fir cone   Cedar cone

Q What is an evergreen tree?

A Some trees have leaves which turn brown and fall off in the winter. Others lose only a few leaves at a time so there are always green leaves on the branches. These are called evergreen trees. One example is the Cedar of Lebanon (above). Some evergreens, such as holly and laurel, have broad leaves, but most have needle-shaped leaves. Because they are not thin and flat, these leaves do not lose moisture as quickly as broad leaves. Most of the needle-leaf trees also grow cones which carry their seeds. They are called coniferous trees and include pine, spruce, fir, cedar and larch.

NATURE

SIMPLE ANIMALS

Q **How does a jellyfish sting?**

A A jellyfish (right) is a bell-shaped sea animal with its mouth underneath. Its body is made of two layers of skin with a jelly-like layer in between. Long tentacles hang down from the body. The tentacles have stinging cells which the jellyfish uses to stun its prey or protect itself from enemies. Humans can sometimes be hurt by these stings. Inside each stinging cell is a coiled thread (inset). When something touches the cell, the thread shoots out, sticking into the prey and injecting venom. In this way, jellyfish can catch large fish.

Q **How many legs has a centipede?**

A A centipede's body is made up of segments. Each segment has one pair of legs attached to it. The centipede in this picture has 18 segments and so it has 36 legs. Some centipedes have only 15 segments and others have as many as 177 segments.

Q **How does an octopus catch its food?**

A An octopus (right) has eight tentacles and hunts on the seabed for fish or shellfish. It creeps towards its prey and then pounces, grabbing hold with its tentacles. Suckers on the tentacles hold the prey firmly while the octopus drags it to its mouth .

Q How does a lobster use its claws?

A A lobster has five pairs of legs, but only uses four pairs for walking. The front pair have developed into large claws or pincers (left). These are very strong and hard. They are used for crushing the shells of molluscs or even for catching small fish. But lobsters do little hunting and usually eat the remains of dead animals on the seabed. Lobsters also use their pincers to shred their food and to fight other lobsters.

Q How are hermit crabs different from other crabs?

A Hermit crabs have hard shells on their front parts, like other crabs, but their abdomens are soft. They live inside the empty shells of other sea animals for protection.

Q Is a starfish really a fish?

A Starfish (below) are not fish but belong to the group of sea animals called echinoderms. The name means 'spiny-skinned'. Starfish have arms, but no head, and no front or back. They move slowly by gripping the seabed with water-filled tubes on their arms. The starfish's arms are so strong that they can pull apart the two shells of a mussel to reach the food inside.

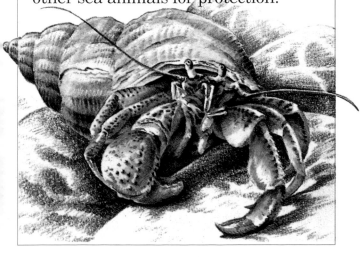

NATURE

INSECTS & SPIDERS

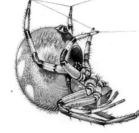

Q How does a spider make a web?

A Spiders make silk in glands near their abdomens. They draw the silk out into threads to build insect traps called webs. The orb spider (right) first fixes threads in a box shape. Then it weaves more threads to the centre. The threads are covered in sticky droplets to catch insects.

Q What is a stick insect?

A Stick insects (right) have long thin bodies with brown or green colouring which makes them look just like the twigs or leaves they sit on. Their enemies, such as birds or lizards, often fail to see them. If they are attacked, stick insects fall to the ground and lie still, once again becoming difficult to see.

Q What is inside an insect?

A An insect's body (right) has many of the organs we have, such as a brain and a heart, but they work differently. Insects breathe through holes called spiracles in their hard outer covering. Their gut is a tube running from the mouth to the end of the abdomen. Their blood runs in an open system throughout the body. All the organs are bathed in blood.

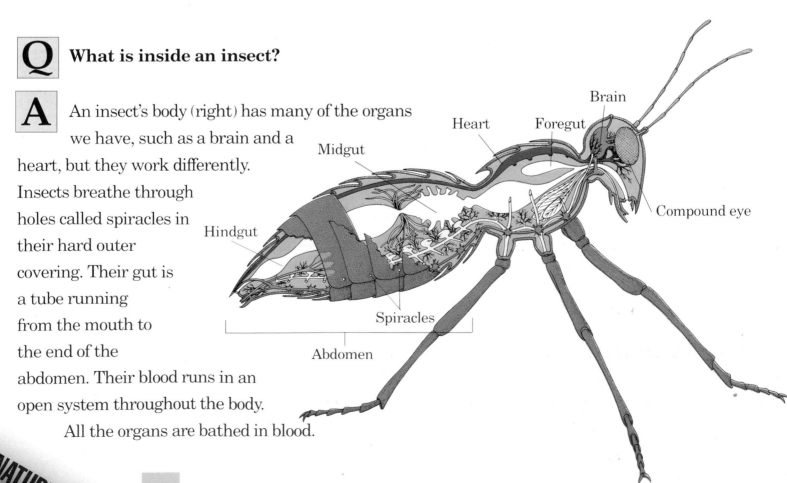

Heart Brain Foregut Midgut Compound eye Hindgut Spiracles Abdomen

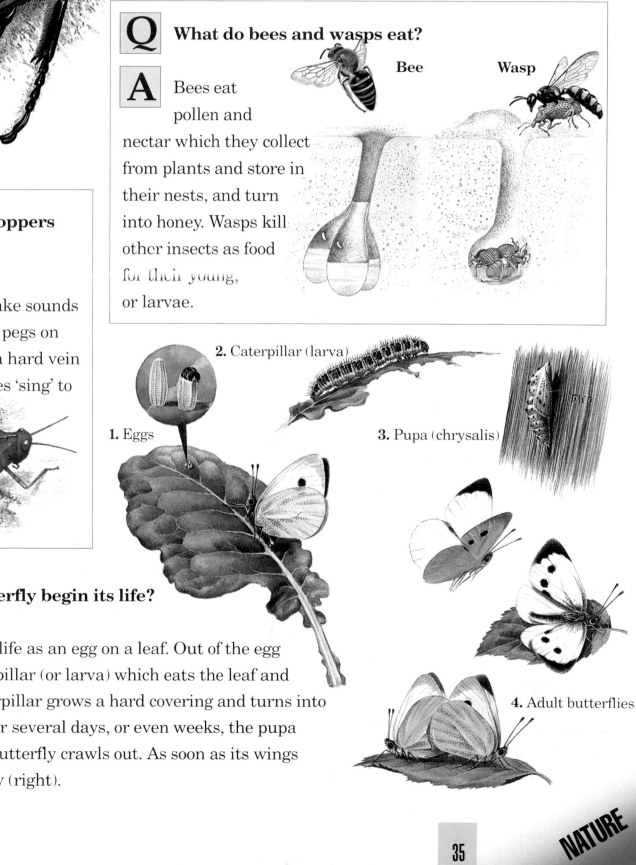

Q Which is the heaviest insect?

A The African Goliath beetle (left) is the heaviest of all insects. It grows as long as 12 cm and weighs up to 110 grams. The lightest insect is the parasitic wasp, the fairy fly, which is less than 0.2 mm long and weighs just 0.006 grams.

Q What do bees and wasps eat?

Bee   Wasp

A Bees eat pollen and nectar which they collect from plants and store in their nests, and turn into honey. Wasps kill other insects as food for their young, or larvae.

Q How do grasshoppers 'sing'?

A Grasshoppers make sounds by rubbing small pegs on their hind legs against a hard vein on their forewings. Males 'sing' to attract a mate.

2. Caterpillar (larva)

1. Eggs

3. Pupa (chrysalis)

Q How does a butterfly begin its life?

A A butterfly begins life as an egg on a leaf. Out of the egg comes a tiny caterpillar (or larva) which eats the leaf and grows very fast. The caterpillar grows a hard covering and turns into a pupa (or chrysalis). After several days, or even weeks, the pupa case splits open and the butterfly crawls out. As soon as its wings have dried, it can fly away (right).

4. Adult butterflies

NATURE

FISH

Q What are the main parts of a fish?

A The main parts on the outside of a fish are the gills (for breathing), the fins (for swimming and steering) and the lateral line (for detecting movement nearby).

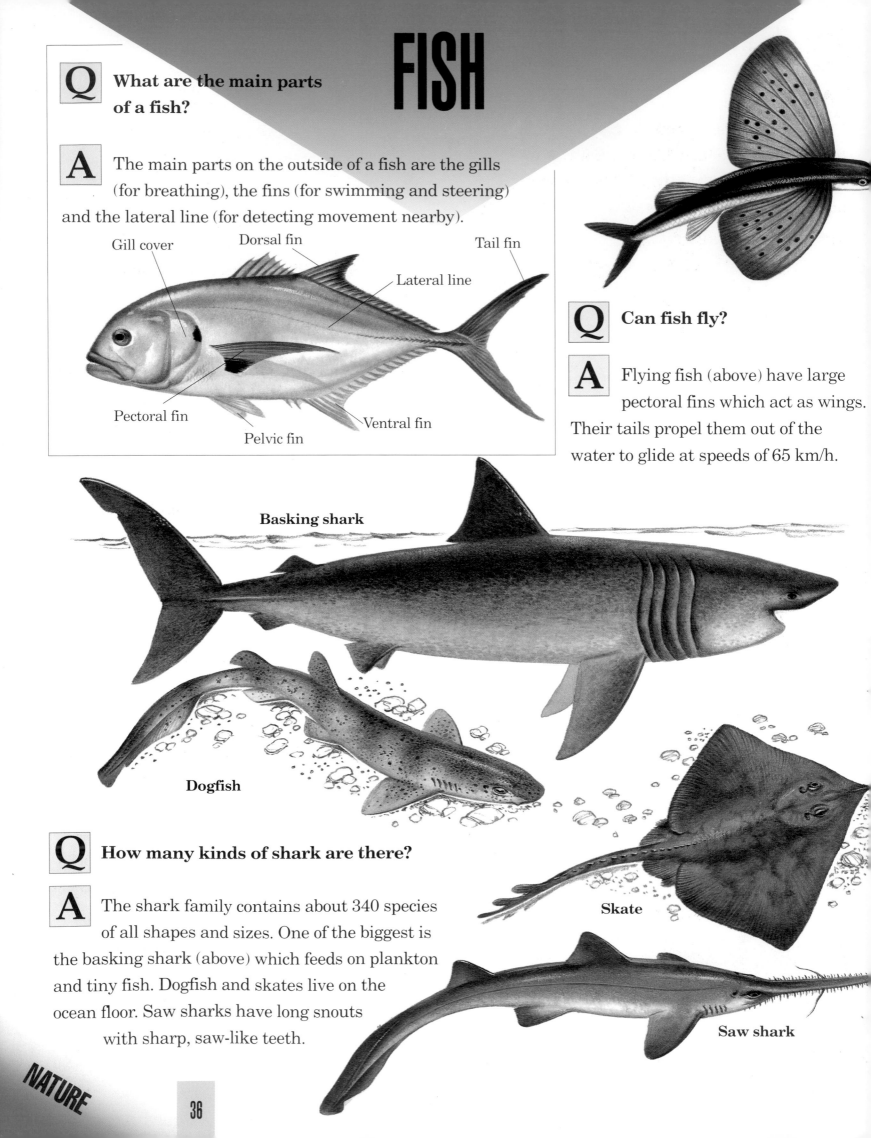

Gill cover

Dorsal fin

Tail fin

Lateral line

Pectoral fin

Pelvic fin

Ventral fin

Q Can fish fly?

A Flying fish (above) have large pectoral fins which act as wings. Their tails propel them out of the water to glide at speeds of 65 km/h.

Basking shark

Dogfish

Q How many kinds of shark are there?

A The shark family contains about 340 species of all shapes and sizes. One of the biggest is the basking shark (above) which feeds on plankton and tiny fish. Dogfish and skates live on the ocean floor. Saw sharks have long snouts with sharp, saw-like teeth.

Skate

Saw shark

NATURE

Q Which fish swims the fastest?

A Sailfish are the fastest swimmers, reaching speeds of up to 109 km/h. The fish's large dorsal fin can lie flat against its body when it is swimming at speed to help streamline it.

Loosejaw

Viperfish

Anglerfish

Hatchetfish

Q What lives at the bottom of the sea?

A It is very dark in the deep sea but many strange fish and other creatures live there. The loosejaw has a huge gaping mouth which traps food. The viperfish is a fierce predator with long, sharp teeth. The hatchetfish has bulging eyes which help it see clearly in the gloom. The anglerfish attracts its prey by waving a shining lure on its snout.

Q Do all fish lay eggs?

A No. Several species, such as the sailfin molly (below), keep their eggs inside until they hatch. Then they give birth to as many as 200 live young.

Q How do cod find their food?

A Some species of fish, such as the Atlantic cod (below) have a single whisker-like projection on their chins to help them feel for their food. This is called a barbel.

NATURE

REPTILES & AMPHIBIANS

Q Where do cobras live?

A The Indian cobra lives in southern Asia. When threatened, it spreads the ribs in its neck, forming a hood. This makes it appear bigger and frightens its enemy. The ringhals is an African cobra. The coral snake, which belongs to the cobra family, lives in the American forests.

Indian Cobra

Ringhals

Coral snake

Q How can a chameleon look in two places at once?

A A chameleon can swivel its eyes separately. One may be looking forwards, and the other backwards. The eyes can also work together to focus on the same object.

Alligator

Crocodile

Q How can you tell the difference between an alligator and a crocodile?

A When a crocodile closes its mouth, the fourth tooth in the lower jaw sticks up outside the top jaw. When an alligator does the same thing, this tooth is hidden.

How do frogs climb trees?

A The tree frog (left) has round discs at the end of its toes. These act as suckers and help the frog to climb up smooth leaves. The toes are long and can curl round thin twigs. Some tree frogs have sticky webbing between their fingers and toes which enable them to hold on more easily. The frog's belly skin is loose and this also clings to the tree.

Q **Why do reptiles flick out their tongues?**

 This monitor lizard (right) is flicking out its tongue. Sometimes the tongue touches the ground, and sometimes it waves in the air. The tongue collects tiny chemical traces and takes them back to the mouth where nerve cells work out what the chemicals mean. By doing this, the monitor can pick up signals about food dangers nearby. Many lizards and snakes use their tongues in the same way.

 How do frogs jump?

A A frog hops and leaps in just the same way as it swims. It lifts its front legs off the ground and pushes off with its powerful back legs (left). The pressure forces open the large webbed feet, giving the frog a firm base from which to jump. It lands on its front legs and chest and then gathers in its back legs, ready for another leap.

BIRDS

Q Which bird sleeps in the air?

A The swift (below) sleeps, feeds and even mates in the air. It is perfectly built for flying. Its long, swept-back wings help it to fly fast and high in the sky, where it hunts for insects. But its legs and feet are weak. It is hard for swifts to hop or walk. Some swifts spend almost all their lives flying.

Q How can owls hunt in the dark?

A The owl (below) listens for the sounds of shrews or mice. It swivels its head until the sound is equally loud in both ears. The owl can then pinpoint exactly where the sound is coming from.

Q How do penguins keep their eggs warm?

A King penguins (right) live near the cold South Pole. The females each lay one egg on the ice in midwinter. The male penguin tucks the egg between his feet and his bulging stomach to keep it warm, until it hatches about two months later.

Q Why do parrots 'talk'?

A In the wild, parrots are sociable birds and call to each other with clicks, squeaks and screams. When they are kept in captivity they sometimes seem to speak like humans. However, the parrots are not really speaking. They are just copying human voices.

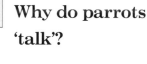

Q **How do hummingbirds feed?**

A Hummingbirds, such as this sword-billed hummingbird, feed on insects and flowers. They poke their long, thin bills and long, tube-like tongues into the flower and suck up the nectar. To do this, the birds have to hover in mid-air. They can beat their wings up to 70 times every second. This makes the humming noise which gives them their name. Hummingbirds can also fly backwards.

Q **Which bird has the widest wingspan?**

A Some species of the albatross (below) can have a 3 metre wingspan – the widest of any bird. The albatross is a sea bird which glides over the waves for hours. It rides on the air currents, rarely flapping its long, narrow wings.

Q **Why do birds have colourful feathers?**

A Most brightly coloured birds are males. Females of the same species may be duller. The males use their colours to attract a mate. Some species, such as the Raggiana bird of paradise (right), display their spectacular feathers by jumping about or even hanging upside down from a branch. The female's dull plumage helps her to hide from danger when she is hatching the eggs.

NATURE

SEA MAMMALS

Q What is the largest animal in the world?

A The blue whale (below) is the largest animal that has ever lived on this planet. It can grow to 27 metres long, and weigh 190 tonnes.

Q Can polar bears swim?

A Polar bears (above) are strong swimmers, and can travel long distances in the icy waters of the Arctic. Their fur is thick and waterproof, and their feet are partly webbed.

Q Which whale can dive the deepest?

A The sperm whale (right) can dive to a depth of more than 3,000 metres. It goes down to the seabed in search of squid to eat. Sperm whales can spend over an hour under water before coming to the surface to breathe.

Q What is a dugong?

A A dugong, or sea cow, is a mammal which lives in the warm waters of the South-west Pacific. It eats sea grasses which it digs up from the shallows. It is a good swimmer, with a flat, forked tail.

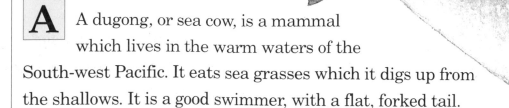

Q What is the difference between a seal and a sea lion?

A Most seals belong to a family called true seals, and sea lions to one called eared seals. Eared seals have small earflaps, but true seals have none. They also swim differently: eared seals mainly use their foreflippers and true seals their hindflippers.

Sea lion

Seal

Q Do whales migrate in winter?

A Yes. The Northern bottlenose whale (right), for example, overwinters in the warm waters off the East African coast in the east, and off New York in the west. In summer, it returns to the North Atlantic.

Q Why do walruses have tusks?

A The tusks of a walrus are the upper canine teeth which grow very long, sometimes to one metre in length. Male walruses (left) usually have longer tusks than females. Walruses use their tusks to scrape up the shellfish and clams they eat, and for gripping the ice, or fighting enemies. Their tusks are also the sign of a walrus' age and importance. The animal with the longest tusks leads the herd.

NATURE

LAND MAMMALS

Q How do bats locate their food?

A Bats (left) have weak eyes, so they use their ears to locate flying insects. They send out high-pitched noises and listen for the echoes. They can tell if the echo comes from an insect, and work out exactly where it is.

Q What is the smallest land mammal?

A The pygmy white-toothed shrew (above) is the smallest mammal which lives on land. It measures only 3.5 cm and weighs about 2 grams. Pygmy shrews live in Africa, and eat spiders, grasshoppers and cockroaches – which may be almost as big as they are.

African elephant   Asian elephant

Q What is the difference between the African and Asian elephant?

A The African elephant is bigger than the Asian, and has larger ears. It also has two lips at the tip of its trunk instead of one.

Q Which is the fastest mammal?

A The cheetah (right) can sprint in short bursts at a speed of nearly 100 kph, faster than any other land animal. It stalks its prey until it is very close, then breaks cover and runs in long, fast strides.

Q How does a camel survive in the desert?

A Camels (right) can go for weeks without drinking. They lose very little water from their sweat or urine. The camel's fur coat protects it from the heat of the Sun, and it can close its nostrils to keep out sand and dust. Wide feet help it to walk over soft sand without sinking. Despite popular belief, camels do not store water in their humps. The humps are used to store fat, which is used for food.

Q Why does a zebra have stripes?

A Some people believe that a zebra's stripes (above) act as a sort of camouflage, making individual animals hard to spot. But now scientists think there are other reasons for the stripes. They may dazzle lions and other cats which attack the zebra. Or they may help the members of a zebra herd to recognize each other.

Q How can you tell a monkey from an ape?

A Monkeys and apes are both primates. Apes, such as the gorilla, have no tails. They have strong arms which are longer than their legs. Most monkeys, like the woolly monkey, have tails with which they can hang from trees.

Woolly Monkey

Gorilla

ECOLOGY

Individual

Population

Community

Ecosystem

Ecosphere

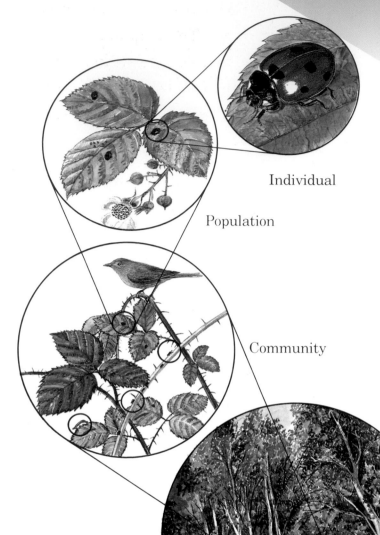

White rhino

Q Why are some animals endangered?

A Today many species of animals are in danger of dying out. They include rhinos (above), whales, wolves, eagles and rain forest birds. Some are being killed because humans want their skins or the land they live on. Others are being poisoned by man-made chemicals or waste products.

Q What is ecology?

A Ecology is the study of plants and animals in their environment (right). Scientists study how individual animals or plants form populations. When these populations live together it is called a community. Different communities form ecosystems (such as a woodland) and ecosystems together are called the ecosphere.

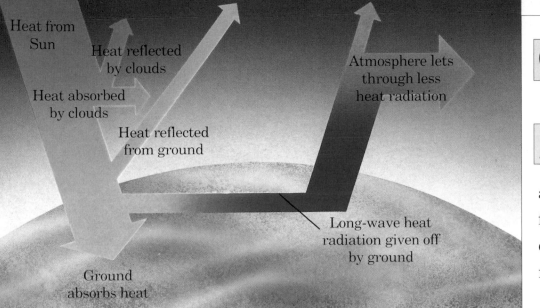

Heat from Sun

Heat reflected by clouds

Heat absorbed by clouds

Heat reflected from ground

Atmosphere lets through less heat radiation

Long-wave heat radiation given off by ground

Ground absorbs heat

Q What is the greenhouse effect?

A Heat comes to the Earth from the Sun. Most of it is then reflected back into space. But some gases trap the heat inside the Earth's atmosphere, which grows very hot like a greenhouse. This is what is known as the greenhouse effect (above).

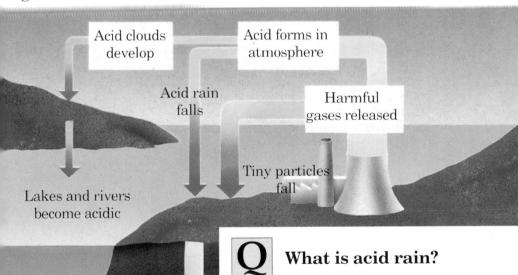

Acid clouds develop

Acid forms in atmosphere

Acid rain falls

Harmful gases released

Tiny particles fall

Lakes and rivers become acidic

Acidic groundwater

Q What is acid rain?

A Factories and power stations release harmful chemicals into the atmosphere. Some, such as sulphur, fall to the ground as tiny particles. The rest are dissolved by the moisture in the atmosphere. When it rains, these chemicals come down, too. This is called acid rain (above). It damages trees and other plants, and poisons the soil. Eventually acid rain drains into rivers and lakes, where it kills many fish.

Q Why are some insects called pests?

A Some insects harm people or crops. The Colorado beetle and the mint-leaf beetle damage food crops. The death-watch beetle destroys timber in buildings. The mosquito carries diseases.

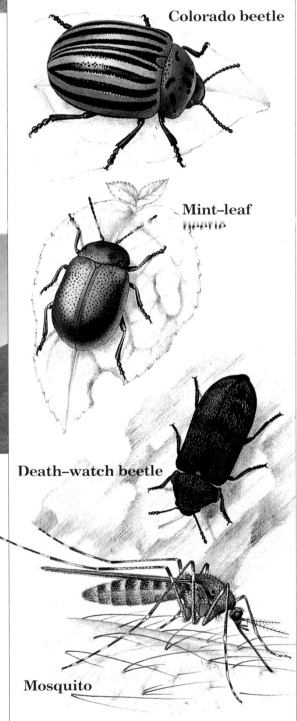

Colorado beetle

Mint–leaf beetle

Death–watch beetle

Mosquito

NATURE

PETS

Q Who were the first people to keep cats as pets?

A The first people to keep cats (right) were probably the ancient Egyptians, over 3,000 years ago. Cats caught the mice, rats and other vermin which raided the grain stores. The cats were well looked after and became pets. In the end, they were worshipped as part of the Egyptian religion. Anyone who killed a cat would be sentenced to death. Some dead cats were even turned into mummies.

Q Why do some rabbits have lop ears?

A This brown and grey lop rabbit has very long, drooping ears. Lops have been specially bred over several centuries by mating does (female rabbits) and bucks (male rabbits) with long ears. Other rabbits (such as chinchillas) are bred to have long fur.

Q Which is the biggest scent hound in the world?

A The biggest of the scent hounds is the bloodhound (right). It has an extremely good sense of smell, more than a million times better than a human's, and is used to track criminals. Hounds are often bred with particular characteristics to help them hunt their prey. Otterhounds, for example, are excellent swimmers and beagles are bred for stamina, enabling them to run long distances.

Otterhound

Beagle

Bloodhound

Q How quickly do mice breed?

A A female mouse is ready to have babies when she is seven weeks old. Three weeks after this, she could give birth to as many as ten young. She may go on producing new litters of babies every 20 to 30 days. In one year, a single mouse could have more than 100 babies!

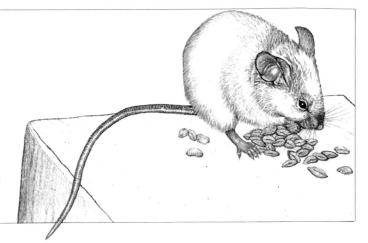

Shubunkin   Common goldfish

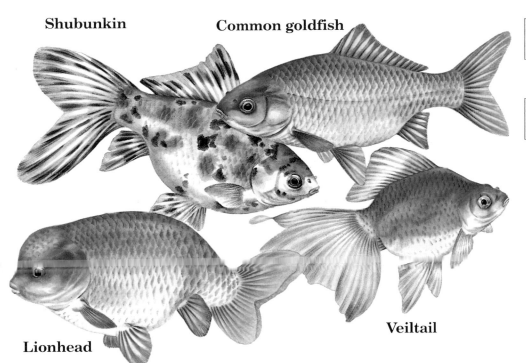

Lionhead

Veiltail

Q How did budgerigars get their name?

A Budgerigars (below) derived their name from the Australian Aboriginals. The Aboriginals like to catch and eat this wild bird so they call it 'betcherrygah', which means 'good cockatoo'. Budgerigars are popular as cage birds. They are brightly coloured and can be taught to mimic the human voice.

Q How many kinds of goldfish are there?

A Goldfish (above) are related to the wild carp. The Chinese have bred carp in ponds for over 2,000 years. They probably picked out the red- and gold-coloured fish and kept them as pets. There are now more than 150 different varieties of goldfish and its close relative, the koi carp. The shubunkin is covered with grey, gold, red or blue patches, with black markings. The common goldfish is very hardy and can live through very cold winters, even if the water ices over. Some goldfish have been bred to have special features. The lionhead has a swelling on top of its head. The veiltail has a long double tail which hangs down like a veil. Other varieties have bubbles on either side of the head, or scales which are almost invisible.

NATURE

Q How can we find out about ancient cities?

 Q What was a ziggurat?

A Archaeologists dig up the ruins of ancient cities (left). They divide the site where the city once stood into squares. Each square is given a number. The archaeologists remember the original position of anything they discover by noting the number of the square they find it in. In this way, they can build up a picture of what the city once looked like.

A A ziggurat was an artificial hill built in a series of layers, or platforms. At the top was a temple. To build a ziggurat (below), huge mounds of clay were strengthened with reeds and covered with bricks. Ziggurats were built in the cities of Mesopotamia from about 2500 BC to 500 BC, and in ancient New World civilizations.

Q Why was Babylon important?

A Babylon (below) stood on the River Euphrates in Mesopotamia (now part of Iraq). At first it was one of a series of small cities. Then Babylon grew in power. By 1700 BC, it controlled an empire, known as Babylonia, which covered the southern part of Mesopotamia. Much of the wealth Babylon gained from the empire was used for building. The Hanging Gardens were a series of irrigated gardens probably built high up on the terraces of a ziggurat.

Q What was the Neolithic?

A This was a period in pre-history (a period where we have no written documents) during which agriculture became a way of life (above). People grew crops of wheat and barley and kept domestic cattle and sheep. Villages were few and scattered, and people rarely travelled more than a few days' walk from home. The Neolithic lasted from about 9000 BC to 3000 BC.

Q What were cylinder seals?

A These were cylinders, generally of stone,

that were used to roll clay over such things as jars, or locks to storehouses, to seal them (right). The cylinders were generally carved with a design. This meant that a pattern was produced when the clay was rolled out. Writing was often carved on to cylinders so that it could be transferred to clay tablets.

Q Who was Solomon?

A Solomon was King of Israel from approximately 970 BC to 922 BC. He was well-known for his immense wealth and wisdom. He encouraged trade and Israel became rich. Solomon extended Israel's empire and started many building schemes, including the building of the first temple at Jerusalem (left), and a palace for himself and his queen.

ANCIENT EGYPT

Q How did the Egyptians use chariots in battle?

A The Egyptian army began to use chariots after 1500 BC. The chariots were made from wood and leather, and were drawn by two horses. They carried two men. While a charioteer drove, a soldier behind would fire arrows at the enemy.

Q What was life like in the Egyptian army?

A The picture below shows the army of Ramesses II, ruler of Egypt from 1290 BC to 1224 BC, in camp. The chariot horses are tethered, and one chariot is being repaired. A band of foot soldiers is being trained. The soldiers are carrying spears and axes with bronze heads, and bows made from two antelope horns tied together. Egyptian soldiers also fought with scimitars, which were curved swords.

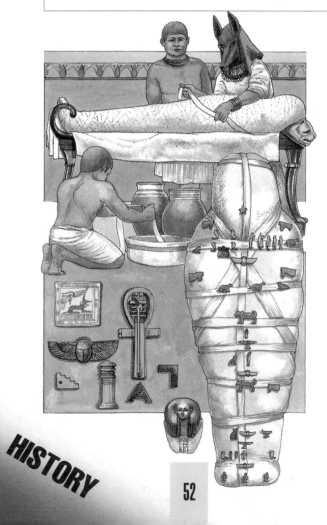

Q What is a mummy?

A The Egyptians believed that people's spirits lived on after death. Because the spirits were attached to the dead body, the body had to be preserved so that it could enjoy the afterlife (left). First, the brain was taken out through the nose, and the heart and other organs were cut out. The body was dried, stuffed with linen and spices, and treated with resin and perfumed oils. Then it was wrapped in linen bandages. At this stage, it was known as a mummy. The chief embalmer wore the mask of Anubis, the jackal god who protected the dead. Small charms called amulets were placed inside the layers of wrappings to protect each part of the body. Finally, the mummies were sealed in grand and costly tombs.

Q What did Egyptian boats look like?

A This boat carried cargoes up and down the River Nile. It had a huge sail, which was wider than it was tall. One man stood in the stern, directing the boat by moving the double steering oars. There were lookout posts at each end of the boat.

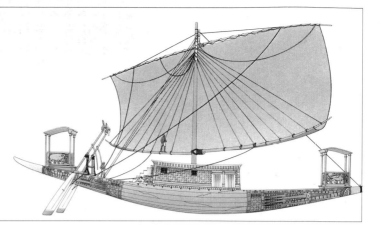

Q What was life like in an Egyptian town?

A Egyptian houses were made of dried mud and built close together (left). Wet mats were spread across the floors to cool the air. Most of the housework, such as cooking and washing, was done outside. People often kept goats and geese in their backyards, as well as pet animals such as dogs, cats and monkeys.

Q How were the pyramids built?

A Between 2630 BC and 1640 BC, Egyptian kings were buried in tombs inside huge pyramids. Stonemasons quarried, shaped and smoothed blocks of stone. The blocks were then lashed to sledges. These were dragged over wooden rollers, which were kept damp to prevent friction. Mudbrick ramps were used to bring the stones up to where they were needed (below).

HISTORY

ANCIENT GREECE

 What did a Greek soldier wear in battle?

 A Greek foot soldier (right) was called a hoplite. He wore a linen shirt with metal armour plates on the shoulders. A bronze breastplate covered his chest and stomach, and greaves (shin guards) covered his legs. He wore a bronze helmet with a tall crest on his head. The hoplite carried a shield and a spear. Round his waist was a belt with a short sword. Hoplites fought in close formation.

 What was the Parthenon?

 The Parthenon (above) was a temple in Athens which honoured the Greek goddess Athena. It was built between 447 BC and 432 BC on a hill called the Acropolis, above the city. The temple had 46 pillars, and was made of white marble. Its ruins still stand today.

 What was a trireme?

 A trireme was a Greek warship (right). It was powered by 170 oarsmen who sat on three levels. Each level had oars of different lengths. The trireme sank enemy ships with a long ram built into its bow.

Q Why was the marketplace important?

A Each city in Ancient Greece had its own government. In the 5th century BC, Athens was the most powerful of these cities, and controlled an empire. Its empire brought Athens trade

and prosperity, and the marketplace became an important part of city life. It was the city's public business area. Here, people would buy the food they needed. It was here, too, that politics might be discussed. Athens was the first ever democracy. This meant that each citizen could participate in how the city was governed. However, only free men who had been born in Athens were counted as citizens.

Q How was Greek pottery made?

A One person would shape the pot by hand (below), while another would paint it. The pots, which were made of clay, were decorated with scenes from daily life, or might show the deeds of gods, goddesses and heroes.

Q What were Greek houses like?

A In the 5th century BC, wealthy Greeks had grand houses made of clay bricks, with stone or tile floors (above). There were separate rooms for eating, cooking, washing and sleeping, built around an open courtyard. The poorer people lived in houses with only one or two rooms.

HISTORY

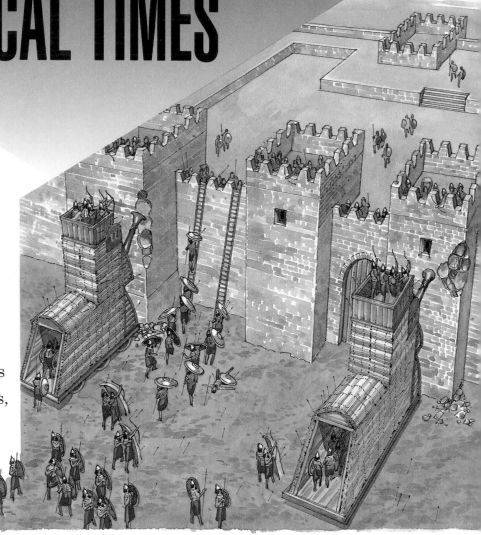

 Where was Canaan?

 Canaan was the land we now know as
Israel. In about 1250 BC, the Israelites,
led by Joshua, invaded Canaan. The
Canaanites were better armed and fought
from horses and chariots (above), but the
Israelites were able to defeat many
Canaanite cities.

 How did Greek culture spread?

 Alexander the Great was king of Greece from 336 BC to
323 BC. He conquered many lands (below), including the
Bible lands of Syria and Egypt. The Hebrews who lived there
began to translate their holy scriptures into Greek.

 Who were the Assyrians?

 These were a people who built
up a powerful empire from
their homeland in Mesopotamia (now
part of Iraq). They were enemies of
the Hebrews from about 860 BC to
612 BC. The Assyrians were skilled in
many areas of warfare. They used
machines such as those shown above
to capture fortified cities. The
machines protected the soldiers while
they knocked down the walls with
battering rams. Other soldiers
distracted the defenders by scaling
the walls with long ladders.

Q Who was Herod the Great?

A Herod was king of Judea (a part of Israel) from about 37 BC to 4 BC. He had a number of palaces built for himself. The largest of these was the Upper Palace in Jerusalem (left), from which Herod governed.

Q Why was the Sea of Galilee important?

A The Sea of Galilee (in Israel) was rich in fish. Fishermen sailed in boats about six metres long. The fish were sold throughout the Roman Empire, bringing wealth to the region.

Q Why were carpenters important in Biblical times?

A Wood was the main material for making tools such as ploughs and yokes (above). Furniture was also made from wood. Jesus and his father, Joseph, are described as carpenters in the Bible.

Q What did Jerusalem look like in Old Testament times?

A Jerusalem (left) was founded some time before 2000 BC. King David made it the Israelite capital in about 1000 BC. Jerusalem was surrounded by strong walls and contained fine palaces, but it remained comparatively small with narrow alleyways and poor housing. King David's son, Solomon, later built a temple and palace in the city.

HISTORY

Bronze coin

Iron nail file

ANCIENT ROME

Centurion

Standard bearer

Gold belt buckle

Bronze oil flask and strigils (scrapers)

Bronze earscoop

Legionary

Q **Which Roman objects are found today?**

A Archaeologists (people who dig up and study ancient objects) often find items (left) near Roman ruins. Metal is found most often because it does not rot easily. Wood, cloth and paper are found only rarely.

Q **How large was the Roman Army?**

A The Roman army had 300,000 men and was very well organized. It was made up of legions, each of 5,500 soldiers called legionaries. A centurion led a group of about 100 legionaries. Each legion had its own standard, like a flag, carried by a standard bearer (right).

Q **How large was the Roman Empire?**

A In AD 211, the Roman Empire covered the land shown on this map (right). About 100 million people lived in the Roman Empire. The lands were divided into areas called provinces. Each province had a governor who collected the taxes, and kept law and order.

- town
- road
- Roman empire AD211

0   800km

0   600mi

Eburacum

Londinium

ATLANTIC OCEAN

Colonia Agrippina

Augusta Treverorum

Moguntiacum

Augusta Vindelicorum

Burdigala

Lugdunum

Poetovio

Apulum

Narbo

Genua

Bononia

Troesmis

Segovia

Tarraco

Salonae

Oescus

Black Sea

Emerita Augusta

Rome

Byzantium

Sinope

Corduba

Thessalonica

Nicomedia

Tingi

Iol Caesarea

Athens

Ephesus

Caesarea

Carthage

Syracuse

Tarsus

Mediterranean Sea

Antiochia

Leptis Magna

Bostra

Cyrene

Caparcotna

Caesarea

Alexandria

Q How did the Romans protect themselves in battle?

A To protect themselves from enemy spears and arrows, Roman legionaries would form a tortoise (below). A group of soldiers would crowd together and lock their shields to form four walls and a roof. It was called a tortoise because it looked like a tortoise's shell.

Roman tortoise

Q What did the Romans build?

Temple

A The Romans were skilful engineers and architects. They built many fine buildings as well as temples to worship their gods. This cross-section through an amphitheatre shows how the arches were designed to carry the enormous weight of the building. The Romans are also famous for their road building.

Amphitheatre

Road

Q What ships did the Romans build?

A The Romans built merchant ships to carry food and other goods, and warships. The merchant ship was broad and deep so that it could carry thousands of containers of goods. The war galley was long and narrow so that it could travel fast and also turn quickly. It used oarsmen as well as sails, so it could move quickly even when there was no wind.

A small warship

A medium-sized merchant ship

HISTORY

MIDDLE AGES

Q Who was buried at Sutton Hoo?

A In AD 625, the Saxon King Raedwald died. He was buried at Sutton Hoo, in Suffolk, England. The king was laid out in a wooden ship, 27 metres long (below), which people believed would take him to the next world. Spears, dishes, coins, armour and a stringed instrument called a lyre were found inside the ship. Also found were silver and gold ornaments, such as these gold clasps (right). The ship and the king were buried under a huge mound of earth. The ship was rediscovered in 1938.

Q What was the Domesday Book?

A William of Normandy conquered England in 1066. In 1086, he ordered a survey of all his English lands to check that he was receiving the rent and taxes to which he was entitled. His officers travelled about the kingdom asking a series of questions, such as the name of each estate and who owned it (right). The answers were written in the Domesday Book. It gives us a detailed picture of what life was like in the Middle Ages.

Q How were cathedrals built in the 12th century?

A During the 12th century, a new style of church architecture was introduced which meant that buildings were much larger and more elaborate than before. This style was known as Gothic architecture (left). The inside of the cathedral was enlarged by building aisles of columns on each side. Arches were built on the outside of cathedrals to support the enormous weight of the roof. Each wall was pierced with windows, which let in light and made the walls lighter.

Q What were the Crusades?

A The Crusades were religious wars fought between the 11th and 13th centuries. They were fought to win back the Holy Lands from non-Christians. The First Crusade began in 1076, when Palestine was captured by Turkish Muslims. The crusading armies were usually led by knights on horseback. Foot soldiers fought with spears and crossbows.

Q What was Paris like in the 14th century?

A The centre of the city of Paris (above) was an island in the River Seine, joined to the rest of the city by bridges. Barges brought goods down the river from all over France. Most houses were made of wood, but the grander buildings were of stone. Grandest of all was the cathedral of Notre-Dame with its twin towers.

HISTORY

EARLY AFRICA

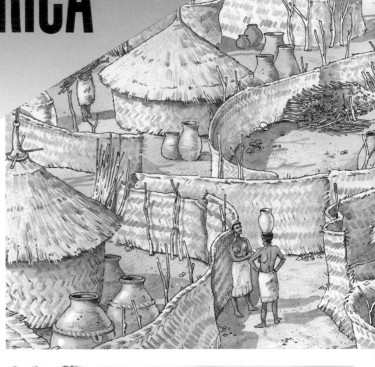

Q Which metals did early Africans use?

A Iron was used in Africa from about 200 BC, and copper from 500 BC. Beautiful statues were a special art form in the Benin Empire (AD 1200-1700) in West Africa. They were cast in bronze or brass. This one (left) shows in detail a hunter returning home. He has an antelope slung over his shoulders with its legs tied.

Q What was the Great Trek?

A In 1806 the British captured the Dutch Cape Colony in southern Africa. Many Dutch farmers, called Boers, resented British rule. In 1836, they set off northeastwards with their families on a Great Trek. They settled north of the Orange and Vaal rivers. The wealthy republics they founded now form part of South Africa.

Q What was Great Zimbabwe?

A The modern state of Zimbabwe (in southern Africa) is named after the ruins of some huge stone-walled enclosures which were found in the hills of south central Zimbabwe. Great Zimbabwe (above) was where the ruler of the city lived, and was the centre of religious life for his people. This is how it would have looked in the 15th century.

Q **What were early African villages like?**

A South of the Sahara, Africa was populated by hundreds of different tribes, each with their own culture. Whatever their way of life, the villages, such as this one in Chad (left), shared much in common. Houses were built from wood, clay or grass. Round huts were very common, each being used for a single purpose such as cooking or sleeping. Huts were usually grouped around a courtyard in which a single family lived. Many Africans still live in traditional villages and huts.

Q **What was the East Coast Trade?**

A The east coast of Africa was for a long time an important source of trade in gold, ivory, slaves and other goods. First to exploit it were the Arabs who sailed as far south as Madagascar from about AD 700 onwards. In 1498 Portuguese ships (right) began to take part in the rich East Coast Trade. Wars were fought between the Arabs and Portuguese for control of ports and sea routes. Other European nations including the Spanish, Dutch and English also exploited the trade.

HISTORY

Q Who were the first people to live in America?

A About 25,000 years ago there was a bridge of land between America and Asia. This was the time of the last ice age. Hunters (below) crossed over from Asia in small bands, following animals such as caribou and bison. Slowly, these settlers spread southwards into the heart of the continent.

Q When did Inuits first live in America?

A Inuits (North American Eskimos) began to move into America from Asia between 4000 BC and 3000 BC. As they travelled, they built temporary houses. In winter, these were made from snow and are called igloos (below).

Q What kind of houses did the Plains Indians live in?

A In the 1400s, many Indians of the Great Plains were farmers. They built large, dome-shaped houses called lodges (right). A lodge had a wooden frame, covered with soil and turf. Entry was through a covered passage. Inside, there was a fireplace in the centre of the lodge. A hole in the roof above let out the smoke. Around the walls were wooden platforms which were used as beds or seats. Before the introduction of the horse by the Spanish, the Plains Indians used dogs for hunting.

HISTORY

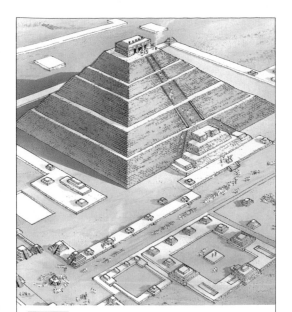

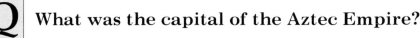

 What was the capital of the Aztec Empire?

 The Aztecs ruled a huge empire in Mexico from AD 1345 to AD 1521. Their capital city was Tenochtitlan, built on swampy islands in Lake Texcoco. Over 300,000 people lived there. Goods were brought to the great markets by a system of canals, and each day vast crowds came to trade. This picture (below) shows the ceremonial centre of the city, with Aztec nobles and warriors. The temple of Quetzalcoatl is before them and, beyond it, the double temple pyramid dedicated to the gods of war and rain.

 What was the Pyramid of the Sun?

 The Pyramid of the Sun was the largest and oldest building in the Mexican city of Teotihuacan, which was built in AD 150. Standing over 70 metres high, the pyramid had a flat roof on which there was probably a temple dedicated to the Sun god.

 How did the Incas travel about their empire?

 The Inca Empire stretched for nearly 4,000 kilometres along the west coast of South America. The Incas built a network of roads across their empire to transport goods, move troops and send messages (left). The roads were made as straight as possible, but zigzagged up steep slopes. Bridges, hung from cables of twisted plant stems, were fixed across ravines and rivers. There were no wheeled vehicles, so most people walked. However, important officers were carried in litters (a type of chair carried on poles).

HISTORY

GREAT EXPLORERS

 Q Where did Christopher Columbus land when he discovered America in 1492?

A Columbus sailed from Spain across the Atlantic in his ship the *Santa Maria* (below). He was trying to reach China. Instead, in 1492, he landed on the island of San Salvador in the Caribbean Sea.

Q Who was Marco Polo?

A Marco Polo was an Italian who travelled from Venice to China with his father and uncle. He arrived in China in 1275 and stayed for 17 years. He worked for the Chinese ruler, Kublai Khan (above). He described his travels in a famous book.

Q Why was Ferdinand Magellan famous?

A In 1519, Ferdinand Magellan, a Portuguese navigator, sailed round the tip of South America, into the Pacific Ocean (right). Magellan himself was killed in 1521, but one of his ships completed the first round the world voyage.

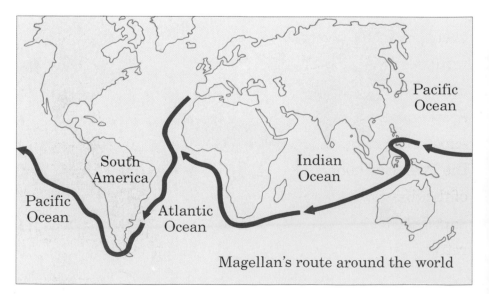

Pacific Ocean

South America

Pacific Ocean

Atlantic Ocean

Indian Ocean

Magellan's route around the world

Q Who was the first European to cross Africa from east to west?

A In 1874, H M Stanley (above) set out with 350 others from Bagamoyo on Africa's east coast. After exploring Lake Victoria, the expedition reached the Congo river. Despite attacks from hostile tribes, they followed the river all the way to the sea on the west coast. The great journey took 999 days. Only 114 people survived.

Q Who led the first expedition to the South Pole?

A Roald Amundsen of Norway landed his party on Antarctica in 1911. Amundsen and four men started for the South Pole on sledges drawn by dogs. They reached the Pole in less than two months (right). The journey back was even quicker and everyone returned safely. Soon afterwards, Robert F Scott's British expedition also reached the Pole. But none of the five men survived the return trip.

HISTORY

INDUSTRIAL REVOLUTION

STEAM ENGINE

CISTERN OF COLD WATER

Q Why were early steam engines important?

A Steam engines allowed industry to develop. The first steam engines were built in the early 1700s. They were used to pump water out of mines. In the 1780s, James Watt produced a steam engine which was much more powerful. This was used to power many machines including spinning and weaving looms, and farm ploughs and threshers.

Q Where was the first steam railway in Britain?

A The very first railway carried goods between Stockton and Darlington in the north of England. It was opened in 1825, and was followed in 1830 by a line between Manchester and Liverpool (right). This carried both goods and passengers.

Q Why was the first seed drill so important?

A Jethro Tull made the first seed drill in 1701. Before this, seed had been scattered by hand. The drill sowed the seed in straight lines (right), so there was less waste and the crop was easier to weed and cut.

Q What was the Industrial Revolution?

A The Industrial Revolution is the name given to a time of great change in Britain. Before the 1700s, people made goods in small quantities, by hand. During the 1700s, machines were invented which made goods much more quickly. Manufacturing industry had begun, and it soon spread around the world. Factories were built (above), and people moved from the countryside to the towns to work in them.

Q Which new goods were made in the Industrial Revolution?

A Machine-woven textiles were produced, so cheap clothes were made. New machines in iron and steel forges enabled pots and pans, rails and other metal goods to be mass-produced. Machine tools such as accurate lathes were invented. With these, goods such as rifles that needed precision-made parts could be produced in factories.

HISTORY

WORLD WARS

Q Who led the Germans during Second World War?

A Adolf Hitler (left) led the Germans during the Second World War (1939-45). His aim was to build a German Empire. In September 1938 he forced Austria to merge with Germany, and Czechoslovakia to hand territory over to him. The following year, he declared war on Poland. This caused Britain and France to declare war against the Germans, but by the end of 1940, France was defeated and Britain isolated. The Americans joined the war against the Germans in 1941, following an attack on Pearl Harbor by Japan (which was allied to Germany), and Germany was finally defeated in 1945.

Q When were aircraft first used in battle?

A Aircraft were used in battle for the first time during the First World War (1914-18). At first they were used to spy on enemy troops, but later guns and bombs were fitted. The triplane (above) was preferred to the biplane as it had greater lift and was easier to manoeuvre.

Q What caused the outbreak of the First World War?

A The murder of the heir to the Austrian throne, Archduke Franz Ferdinand, on 28th June 1914, finally started the First World War (1914-18). He was killed by a Serb, causing Austria to declare war on Serbia.

Q What was trench warfare?

A During the First World War, soldiers dug trenches (below) as protection against weapons such as machine guns and heavy artillery. Soldiers would live in the trenches for weeks on end. Attacks were often made from the trenches.

Q What sort of weapons were used in the Second World War?

A Aircraft played a decisive role in many battles, while armoured tanks made land warfare highly mobile. Aircraft carriers enabled aircraft to attack from the sea.

Tank

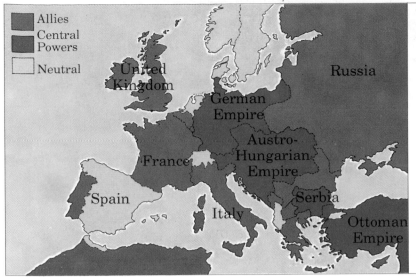

Allies
Central Powers
Neutral

United Kingdom
Russia
German Empire
France
Austro-Hungarian Empire
Spain
Serbia
Italy
Ottoman Empire

Q What were the main alliances during the First World War?

A The two main alliances during the First World War were those who fought with the German Empire (known as the Central Powers), and those who fought against the German Empire (known as the Allies). Neutral countries did not fight on either side.

Q What was D-Day?

A D-Day was a code name used in the Second World War. It was the name given to the date when 130,000 troops from the British and American armies were due to land in France and liberate it from the Germans (right). The date was changed several times due to bad weather, but D-Day eventually took place on 6th June 1944.

Spitfire

Stuka

Aircraft carrier

HUMAN BODY

Epidermis

Hair

Oil gland

Nerve endings

Dermis

Sweat gland

Q What is the skin for?

A The skin (above) is the protective outer covering of our body. It contains nerve endings, which detect pain; sweat glands, which keep the body cool; and hair. It also prevents the body from losing too much water.

Q How do muscles work?

A There are more than 600 muscles in the body (right). Most of them move parts of the body or help it to stay upright. Muscles cannot push, they can only pull. Many of them work in pairs, attached to bones by tendons. One muscle tightens and becomes shorter, pulling the bone after it. If it relaxes, and the other muscle tightens, the bone moves back.

Q How many bones do we have?

A Humans have 206 bones in their bodies (right). There are 29 in the skull, 26 in the spine, 32 in each arm, and 31 in each leg. Other bones form the ribcage.

Skull

Collar bone

Ribcage

Pelvis

Spine

Femur (thigh bone)

Tibia and Fibula (shin bones)

Chest muscles used in breathing

Neck muscles turn head

Upper arm muscles bend and straighten elbow

Q What is inside a bone?

A Bones are not solid. They have a strong outer layer of compact bone, with lightweight, spongy bone inside. In the centre is the soft marrow, which makes new red cells for the blood.

Blood Vessel

Compact bone

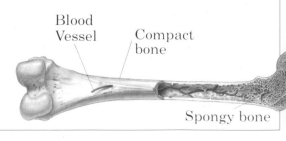

Spongy bone

Q What are veins and arteries?

A When blood leaves the lungs, it carries oxygen. This blood travels along vessels called arteries. The body absorbs the oxygen, and the blood travels back to the heart through veins (below).

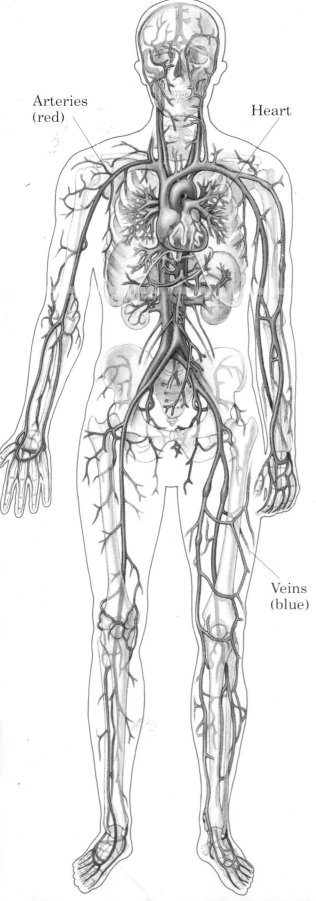

Arteries (red)

Heart

Veins (blue)

Q How does the heart work?

A The heart is a muscular pump. Oxygen-rich blood from the lungs enters the left side of the heart and is pumped to the organs. Veins carry the blood back to the right side of the heart. The blood is then pumped back to the lungs.

Right atrium

Left atrium

Left ventricle

Right ventricle

Q How do our joints work?

A Joints are the places where bones move against each other. Shoulders and hips have ball and socket joints. These allow movement in any direction. Elbows have hinge joints, which allow them to move backwards and forwards. A pivot joint allows the head to turn sideways.

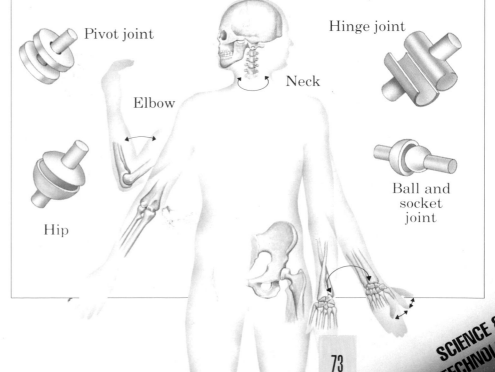

Pivot joint

Hinge joint

Neck

Elbow

Ball and socket joint

Hip

SCIENCE & TECHNOLOGY

SENSES & ORGANS

Q How do we breathe?

A Our bodies need oxygen, which they get from air breathed into the lungs. The lungs are made to expand by a big muscle called the diaphragm, and smaller muscles fixed to the ribs. The diaphragm pushes downwards, while the other muscles lift up the rib cage. This draws air down into the lungs, where the oxygen is absorbed into the blood stream (right).

Air breathed in through nose and mouth

Oesophagus

Lungs

Trachea

Bronchus

Diaphragm

Q Where does our food go?

A After the teeth chew the food, it is swallowed and goes down the oesophagus into the stomach (below). It is mixed with digestive juices, which break it down. In the small intestine, nutrients from the food are absorbed. Waste matter leaves the body through the anus.

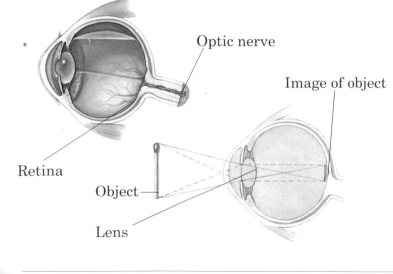

Mouth

Oesophagus

Liver

Stomach

Small intestine

Large intestine

Anus

Q How do our eyes see?

A When we look at something, light from it enters our eyes. The light is focused on the retina at the back of the eye by the lens. The optic nerves in the retina send a message to the brain, enabling us to 'see'.

Optic nerve

Image of object

Retina

Object

Lens

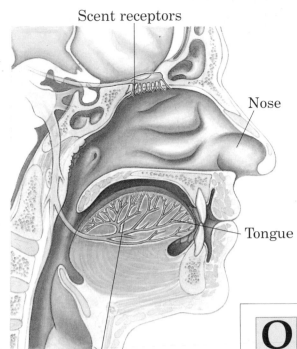

Scent receptors

Nose

Tongue

Taste receptors

Q How do we taste and smell?

A In the upper part of the nose are tiny scent receptors (left). When we sniff, molecules in the air are carried to these receptors. They sense what we are smelling. The tongue is covered with about 9,000 taste receptors, or taste buds. These sense what we are tasting. The taste buds are grouped in special areas on the tongue. Sweetness is tasted at the front, saltiness and sourness at the sides, and bitterness at the back.

Q How do our ears work?

A The outer ear collects sound waves, which pass through the eardrum and vibrate the tiny bones in the middle ear. These vibrations set the fluid in the cochlea in motion, shaking tiny hairs. Nerves attached to the hairs pass the message to the brain.

Middle ear

Outer ear

Ear bones

Eardrum

Cochlea

2 weeks

4 weeks

6 weeks

8 weeks

Q How does a baby develop during pregnancy?

A A baby's life begins when a male sperm joins a female egg. The sperm travels from a man into a woman's body. It joins with the egg to form a single cell, and starts to grow. After a week, the single cell has multiplied to more than 100 cells. After eight weeks, the baby has all its major organs (such as heart, liver and lungs). The baby gets its food from its mother through the umbilical cord. After nine months, the baby is about 50 centimetres long (left). It is ready to be born.

Baby

Uterus

Umbilical cord

Plant cell

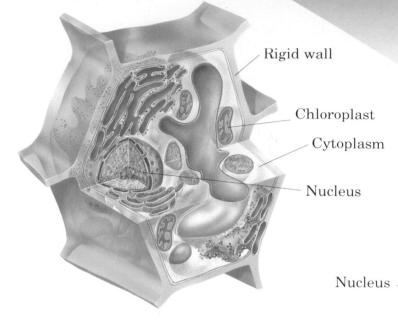

Rigid wall

Chloroplast

Cytoplasm

Nucleus

Non-rigid wall

Animal cell

Nucleus

Cytoplasm

Q Why do animals of the same species fight?

A Animals fight others of their species for several reasons. They may be arguing over territory, or the right to be leader of their herd. Although many animals have powerful weapons, such as teeth, horns or claws, few are ever killed in these contests. These two klipspringer antelopes are jabbing at each other with their sharp horns.

Q What is a cell?

A A cell (above) is the basic building block of almost every living thing. Plant cells have a rigid wall made from a material called cellulose. Animal cells do not have a rigid wall. Inside all cells is a fluid called cytoplasm, containing the nucleus and other small bodies. The nucleus is the cell's control centre. The chloroplasts in plant cells help trap the energy from sunlight. The energy is used to turn carbon dioxide and water into food for the plant.

Q How do plants make seeds?

A Plants have male and female parts that join together to make seeds. A pollen grain travels from the male anther of one flower to the female stigma of another (right). The pollen is usually carried by an insect or the wind. It fertilizes an egg in the ovary, which becomes an embryo and then a seed. The seed will grow into a new plant.

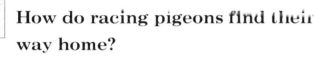

Anther

Pollen

Stigma

Pollen tube

Seed

Ovary

Embryo

Q Do animals live in families?

A Some animals live together in herds or flocks, but others live in small family groups. This is a family of tamarin monkeys (above). The older brothers and sisters carry and help groom the babies.

Q How do racing pigeons find their way home?

A Racing pigeons and many other species of birds probably use more than one way of navigating. They can find their direction from the position of the Sun by day and the stars by night. They can also detect changes in the Earth's magnetic field as they fly over it. This tells them whether they are flying north, south, east or west. Some birds find their way by smell.

Q How do birds fly?

A These pictures (below) show a duck beating its wings once as it flies. The downstroke (left) lifts the bird up and propels it forward. On the upstroke (right) the feathers are opened to let air through.

ENERGY

Q What is hydroelectricity?

A A hydroelectric plant (below) uses water to make electricity. The water is stored behind a dam, and flows rapidly down to a turbine. The force of the water turns the turbine shaft. This drives the generator, which makes electricity. Hydroelectric plants are cheap to run and cause little pollution.

Glass

Copper tubing

Cold water

Hot water cylinder

Warm water

Dam wall

Reservoir

Turbine   Generator

Q How can we store the Sun's heat?

A The Sun can be used to heat water inside the copper tubing in a solar panel (above). This is then carried to a hot water cylinder to be stored for later use.

Q How do we reach oil that is under the sea?

A Oil often lies beneath several layers of rock. First a number of holes, or wells, are drilled down to the oil (right). A production platform is fixed above the wells and the oil is pumped up. From the platform, the oil is pumped through the loading buoy to the waiting tankers.

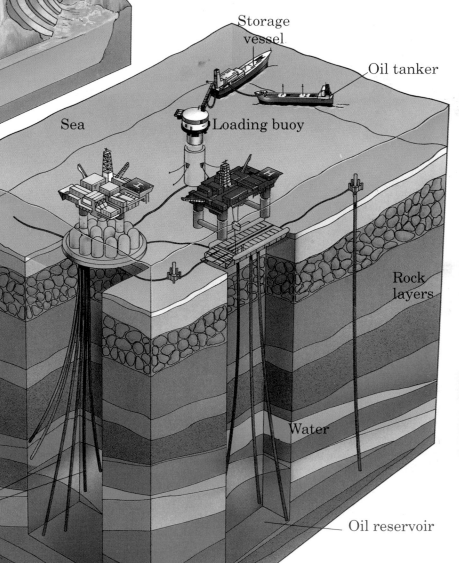

Storage vessel

Oil tanker

Sea

Loading buoy

Rock layers

Water

Drilling pipes

Oil reservoir

Q How does electricity travel to our homes?

A Electricity is generated at a power station (below). The station burns fuel to heat water into steam. The steam turns a turbine which causes a generator to produce electricity. The used steam is condensed back to water. This water is then cooled in the cooling tower. The electric current passes through a transformer, which increases the current to about 750,000 volts. Then power lines, strung from tall pylons, carry the current to houses and factories. Factories need high-voltage electricity for manufacturing. But the current is too high for most other users. It passes through a series of substations. Here, transformers lower the voltage. Smaller factories may use currents of between 2,000 and 12,000 volts. Street lights and traffic signals use less. For homes, shops and offices the current is lowered to about 240 volts.

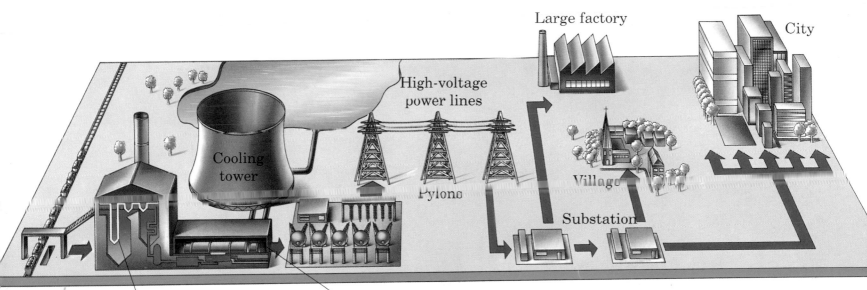

Large factory — City — High-voltage power lines — Cooling tower — Pylons — Village — Substation — Furnace and boiler — Transformer

Q What is coal made from?

A Coal is the remains of plants which died millions of years ago, during the Carboniferous period (right). These became buried under mud and slowly dried out to form peat. More layers of clay and gravel squashed the peat still further. Eventually the weight of this and other dead material compressed the bottom layers into the hard, black, shiny substance we call coal (far right).

SCIENCE & TECHNOLOGY

ATOMS & MOLECULES

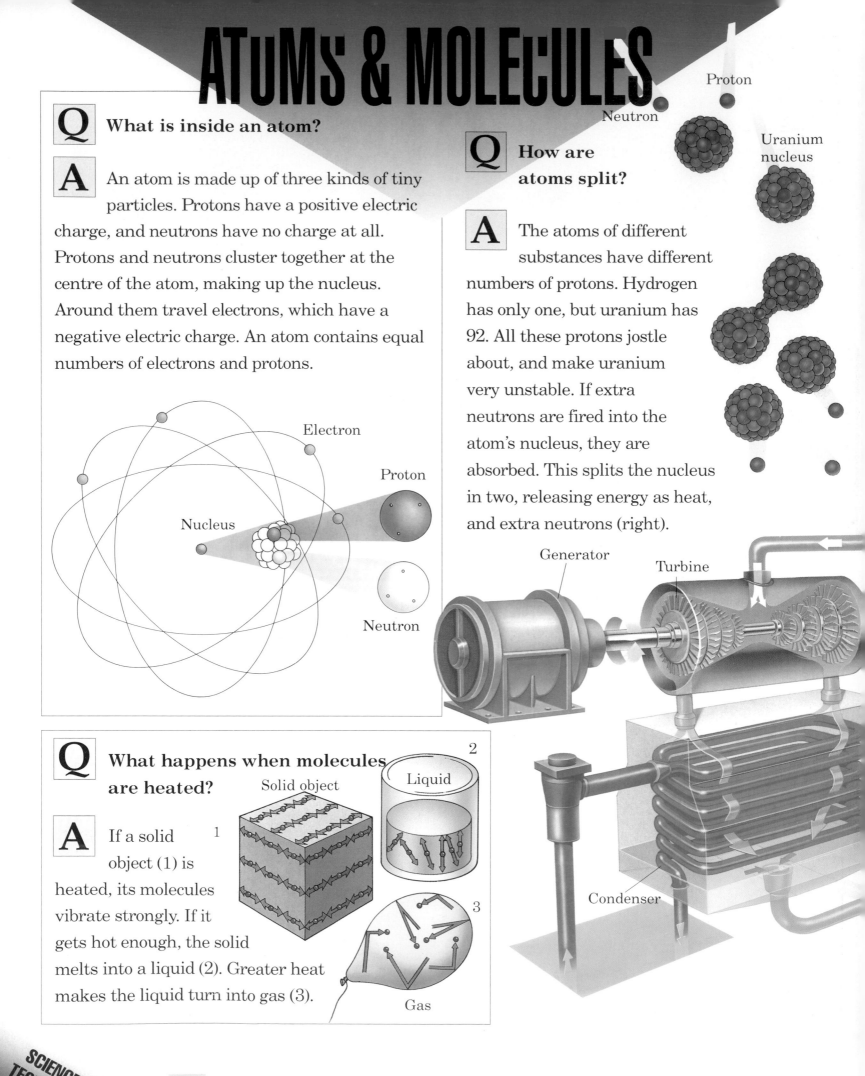

Q What is inside an atom?

A An atom is made up of three kinds of tiny particles. Protons have a positive electric charge, and neutrons have no charge at all. Protons and neutrons cluster together at the centre of the atom, making up the nucleus. Around them travel electrons, which have a negative electric charge. An atom contains equal numbers of electrons and protons.

Electron

Proton

Nucleus

Neutron

Q How are atoms split?

A The atoms of different substances have different numbers of protons. Hydrogen has only one, but uranium has 92. All these protons jostle about, and make uranium very unstable. If extra neutrons are fired into the atom's nucleus, they are absorbed. This splits the nucleus in two, releasing energy as heat, and extra neutrons (right).

Proton

Neutron

Uranium nucleus

Generator

Turbine

Condenser

Q What happens when molecules are heated?

A If a solid object (1) is heated, its molecules vibrate strongly. If it gets hot enough, the solid melts into a liquid (2). Greater heat makes the liquid turn into gas (3).

Solid object

1

Liquid

2

3

Gas

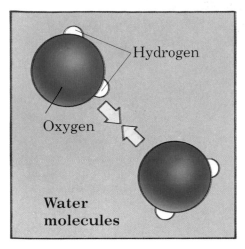

Water molecules

 What is a molecule?

A A molecule is the smallest part of a substance. Its atoms are linked chemically. Two hydrogen atoms and one oxygen atom make a water molecule (left).

Q How can we use the energy from atoms?

A When a uranium atom is split, its releases neutrons which shoot off into surrounding atoms and split them, too. This splitting carries on in what is called a chain reaction. It gives out a lot of energy in the form of heat, which can be used to generate electricity in a nuclear power station (left). Rods of uranium are placed inside the reactor. Control rods made of steel are put between the uranium rods to control the reaction. Water is pumped through the reactor under pressure and absorbs the heat. This water is carried to the steam generator, where its heat is used to boil a separate supply of water into steam. The steam is fed to a turbine. It spins the turbine, which turns the generator and so produces electricity. The used steam then travels to the condenser, where it is turned back into water and fed back to the steam generator to be re-used.

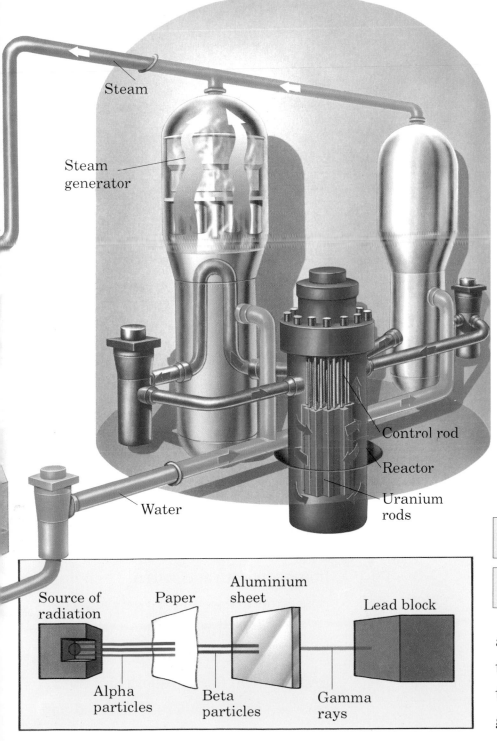

Steam

Steam generator

Water

Control rod

Reactor

Uranium rods

Q What are the types of radiation?

A There are three types of radiation – alpha, beta and gamma. Alpha particles are the least powerful. They cannot pass through paper. Beta particles cannot pass through thin metal, such as aluminium, and gamma rays cannot pass through lead (left).

Source of radiation

Paper

Aluminium sheet

Lead block

Alpha particles

Beta particles

Gamma rays

SCIENCE & TECHNOLOGY

INDUSTRY

 How is plastic made into shapes?

 In blow moulding, a piece of hot plastic tubing is placed in a mould. Air is blown into the tube, pushing it out into the shape of the mould.

Blow moulding

In vacuum moulding, plastic is placed over a mould and heated. Air is removed, and the vacuum pulls the plastic into the mould.

Vacuum moulding

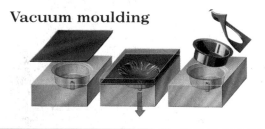

 How is coal mined?

 Most coal is mined by either the 'longwall' or 'room-and-pillar' method (right). In longwall mining a giant coal cutter runs down the coal face removing coal as it goes. In room-and-pillar mining the coal is removed from chambers, but pillars of coal are left behind to support the roof.

Room-and-pillar mining

Coal seam

Coal cutter

Longwall mining

Roof supports

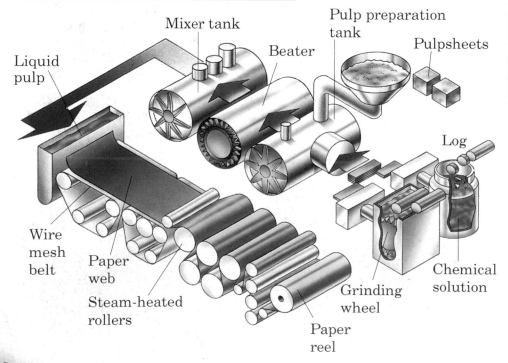

Mixer tank

Beater

Pulp preparation tank

Pulpsheets

Liquid pulp

Log

Wire mesh belt

Paper web

Steam-heated rollers

Grinding wheel

Paper reel

Chemical solution

Q What is paper made from?

A Most paper is made from wood (left). The wood is ground up or mashed into pulp using chemicals. The pulp is beaten so that the tiny wood fibres separate and soften. Then it passes on to a belt of wire mesh. The water drains through the mesh, and the pulp (now called the web) is squeezed first between heavy rollers and then between heated rollers. The dried and finished paper is wound on to reels.

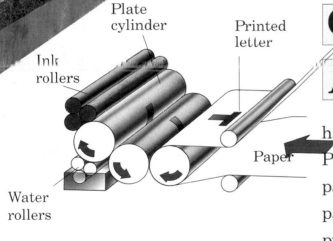

Shaft

Ventilation shaft

Conveyor belt

Coal carried to surface

Q How is cloth made on a loom?

A A loom is a machine that joins together two yarns (long threads) in a criss-cross pattern, to make a cloth. The warp yarn is strung along the loom (below). The threads are raised and lowered, forming a gap or 'shed'. Then a shuttle carrying the weft yarn is passed through the shed. Yarns can be woven into many different patterns.

Warp yarn

Shuttle

Weft yarn

Loom

Satin weave

Plain weave

Sateen weave

Twill weave

Plate cylinder

Printed letter

Ink rollers

Water rollers

Paper

Q How is a newspaper printed?

A Newspapers are printed by offset lithography. The plate cylinder has a pattern of the parts to be printed. Paper is fed through rollers, and the pattern printed with ink. The other parts are treated with water to prevent the ink marking them.

Iron ore mixed with limestone and coke

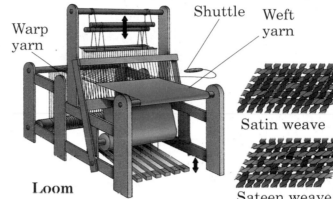

Q How is iron extracted from iron ore?

A Iron ore contains other substances as well as iron. The iron is extracted in a tall tower called a blast furnace (right). The ore, mixed with limestone and coke, is fed through the top. Then very hot air is blown in through pipes at the bottom of the furnace. The iron melts, and the other materials rise to the top as slag. The iron is drained off from the bottom.

Liquid iron drained off

Hot blast stoves

Hot air blasted in

SCIENCE & TECHNOLOGY

Q How does a digital watch work?

A Tiny quartz crystals inside the digital watch (right) vibrate at a steady rate when an electric current from a battery is applied. A silicon chip picks up the vibrations and turns them into regular pulses. The pulses are displayed as numbers on the liquid crystal display (LCD) on the watch face.

LCD

Vibration

Battery

Lens

Button to open shutter

Shutter

Film

Q How does a camera work?

A When the camera's shutter is opened, light passes through a lens on to the film (above). The film is covered with chemicals which store the pattern as a photograph.

Fan

Electric motor

Elements

On/Off Switch

Q How do hairdriers blow out hot air?

A A hairdrier (above) uses electricity in two different ways. When you switch it on, a small electric motor turns a fan inside. The fan sucks in air from the back of the hairdrier, and blows it out at the front. As the air travels through the hairdrier, it passes over a set of wire coils called elements. These are heated by the electricity, warming the air as it passes.

Q How does a vacuum flask keep liquids hot?

Cup
Stopper

A Inside a vacuum flask are two glass bottles, one inside the other. They are sealed together at the top. The air between the two bottles is removed to form a vacuum. This helps to stop the heat escaping. The insides of the bottles are painted silver. This reflects the heat from the liquid inside the flask.

Vacuum

Q What is inside a video camera?

A The lens at the front of a video camera (left) is automatically focused by an infrared beam. The vidicon tube converts the image into electric impulses. These pulses are recorded on the video tape. At the same time the microphone picks up the sound, which is recorded on the edge of the video tape.

Microphone

Canon

MIC

EVF

Lens

Video tape

Vidicon tube

Infrared beams

Q Why do bicycles have gears?

Gear lever

Pedal

Cog wheel

Chain

A Gears allow a cyclist to pedal at a steady rate, even when climbing hills. The gear lever lifts the chain from one cog wheel to another. Large cog wheels turn slowly, making it easier to cycle uphill. Small cog wheels turn quickly, making it easier to pedal downhill.

Digital thermometer

Digital display

Scale

Mercury

Liquid thermometer

Q How do thermometers work?

A A liquid thermometer contains a liquid metal, mercury. When the temperature goes up, the mercury expands and rises in the tube. A digital thermometer has an electronic circuit, which displays the temperature digitally.

COMPUTERS

Micro circuit

Q Can robots do the same things as people?

A Robots can perform many of the routine tasks carried out by people in factories and workshops (right). Different types of robot can be used for jobs such as welding or painting. Robots work without tiring, but can only repeat the task they have been programmed to perform.

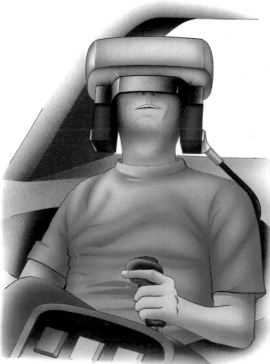

A Smart cards (above) are used by banks and other organizations. Inside the small piece of plastic is a micro circuit on which information is stored. A smart credit card, for instance, has money values stored in it which are reduced every time a purchase is made. Phone cards are a simple form of smart card.

Pick-and-place robot

Q What is virtual reality?

A Virtual reality is a computerized fantasy world which seems like the real thing. To enter it, the user wears a helmet with a computer screen inside (right). As he moves his head, he appears to see different parts of the 'world' within the screen. In some virtual reality programs the user moves a joystick to make the images move on the screen. Sometimes sensors attached to the body enable the user to 'touch' things. The science of virtual reality is still at an early stage. It takes powerful computers to run even a simple program. Simulators used to train aircraft pilots and tank commanders use a form of virtual reality.

What are computer peripherals?

A Computer peripherals (left) are devices which input or output computer information. For example, a keyboard may be used to type in information. A mouse, joystick or light-pen can also be used to give instructions. Information can be stored in the computer itself or on floppy disks.

Plotter

Visual display unit (VDU)

Joystick

Keyboard

Printer

Light-pen

Mouse

Floppy disks

 What is computer-aided design?

A Computer-aided design is often used in industry. Details of a new product design are fed into a computer. The computer displays a model which designers can look at from all angles. They can test out new ideas on the model. For instance, the addition of a more powerful engine may require wider tyres. Here (right) a computer model is being used to test air flow over a car design. This shows that the addition of a small spoiler on the rear of the car will give better road holding.

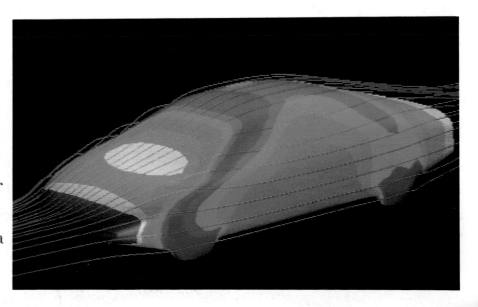

SCIENCE & TECHNOLOGY

Q Which is the fastest passenger train?

A The French TGVs are the fastest passenger trains (right). TGV stands for 'Train à Grand Vitesse' which means 'very fast train'. TGVs regularly travel at speeds of up to 270 km/h on special sections of track which are as straight and flat as possible. They are powered by electricity from overhead wires. Each train has a power unit at the front. This has a streamlined nose to cut down wind resistance.

 Q How big is an oil tanker?

A Oil tankers (right) carry crude oil and oil products. Supertankers can carry hundreds of thousands of tonnes of oil. The largest supertanker was over 566 metres long and 69 metres wide. When it was fully loaded with petroleum, 24 metres of its hull were under water. Supertankers are difficult to steer, and so heavy that they can take up to five kilometres to stop completely.

Tug used to help tanker dock

Q What is an articulated truck?

A An articulated truck (right) is one which consists of two separate parts. At the front is the part called the tractor unit, which contains the diesel engine, the controls, the fuel tank and the driver's cab. It has very powerful brakes and some have more than 20 gears. The tractor unit pulls the part called the trailer, which carries the cargo.

Q What is a 'supersonic' airliner?

A Supersonic means faster than the speed of sound. The speed of sound is measured as 1,200 km/h at sea level. Concorde (left) is the only airliner capable of flying at supersonic speed. It can reach 2,100 km/h. Other commercial aircraft are not designed to fly at supersonic speed; the shock waves and buffeting which would occur as they approached this speed would destroy the aircraft.

Q Who built the first steam railway locomotive?

A In 1804, Richard Trevithick built the first successful steam engine to run on rails. It hauled trucks of coal along a tramway in South Wales, UK. Trevithick later built a locomotive called 'Catch me who can', which travelled at speeds of up to 16 km/h.

SCIENCE & TECHNOLOGY

CARS

Q How is a modern car built for safety?

A A modern car has complex machinery and structures built into the bodywork so that it is safe (left). A strong body frame is designed to protect the occupants in a crash. An anti-lock braking system (ABS) enables the car to brake without skidding by releasing and reapplying the brakes many times every second. The steering column is made in sections that will collapse in the event of a crash.

Body frame

Tyre

Steering column

3. Body checked for alignment

2. Body welded

1. Floor pan pressed from steel sheet

7. Paint dried

4. Final body welding

8. Body finished

5. Undercoat paint applied

6. Colour paint applied

Q How are cars made?

9. Engine assembled

10. Electrical and cooling systems fitted

A Most cars are manufactured on production lines (right). The vehicle is placed on an assembly platform which moves slowly through the factory. At each stage along the line, workers or robots gradually complete the car.

11. Interior, doors and wheels fitted

12. Tests carried out

Q Why do car engines need oil?

A As a car travels, many of its parts move
against each other. The different parts of the
engine (right) move at high speed. Oil is pumped
from the sump to lubricate the bearings, pistons
and other components, allowing the metal parts to
move without causing wear or generating heat
through friction. Some vehicles use special oils if
they are to be used in very cold conditions.

Filler cap   Camshaft   Cylinder

Drive belt

Fan

Crankshaft

Oil filter

Oil sump

Pump

Fuel in

Air in

Injector

Exhaust

Spark plug

Cylinder

Q What is fuel injection?

A Car engines burn fuel
in closed cylinders. A fuel
injection system pumps a precise
amount of fuel into the cylinders as air is
sucked in (above). The mixture is then
ignited by a spark plug and the waste
gases flow through the exhaust.

Q What did the first cars look like?

A The first cars were
built in the 1880s. To
begin with, engines were
built into carriages normally pulled by horses. These
'horseless carriages' had simple controls.

Q How are racing cars designed to go fast?

A Most modern cars are
designed for comfortable travel. Racing cars
(right), however, are designed for speed. They are very light,
but strong, and the powerful engines are designed to accelerate
extremely fast. The tyres are wide so they grip the road extremely
well. The bodywork is designed to reduce air resistance and special
fins are added to improve handling and road holding.

Engine

Extra wide
tyres

SCIENCE & TECHNOLOGY

FARMING

Q How does a combine harvester work?

A A combine harvester (right) does nearly all the jobs in harvesting a cereal crop. At the front is the big pick-up reel. This pulls the crop into the cutter bar. The cut cereal is pushed by a rotating screw on to an elevator, which takes it to the threshing cylinder. This rotates very fast and separates the grain from the stalks. The grain is stored in a bin. When the bin is full, the grain is unloaded into a truck. The stalks are pushed out of the back of the harvester on to the ground.

Stalks

Grain

Threshing cylinder

Elevator

Pick-up reel and cutter bar

Rotating screw

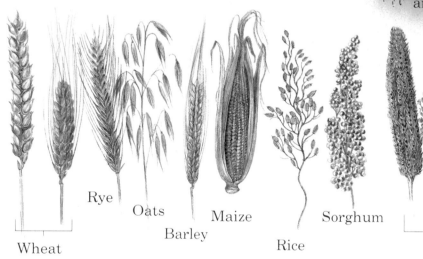

Rye

Oats

Barley

Maize

Rice

Sorghum

Millet

Wheat

Q Which plants are the most important source of food?

A Cereals are plants which produce grains (above). They are our most important source of food. The most common cereal is wheat. It is used to make bread or pasta and is the staple food of more than a third of the world's people. Rye, oats and barley are grown in northern Europe, mainly as animal food. Maize (corn) is a major crop in America and Africa, and rice is the staple grain of Asia. Sorghum and millet are also grown in Asia and Africa.

Q What is the cotton plant used for?

A The cotton plant grows in many of the warm parts of the world. The fibres which grow around the seeds are used to make cloth. The seeds are crushed to produce vegetable oil, or to make cattle food or fertilizers.

Q Why are there so many types of cattle?

A There are more than 200 breeds of cattle throughout the world. Many, such as this Friesian cow (right), are kept in herds to produce milk. Others, such as the Hereford, are raised for their meat. The hardy Zebu is best suited to the hottest parts of India and Africa.

Q Which products are made from milk?

A Milk has many uses. From the cow, it is pumped into the farm vat and then taken by tanker to the dairy. Here the milk is pasteurized (heated to kill the bacteria). If it is to be used for drinking, it is sealed into bottles or cartons. Milk can also be processed and turned into yoghurt, cheese, cream and butter.

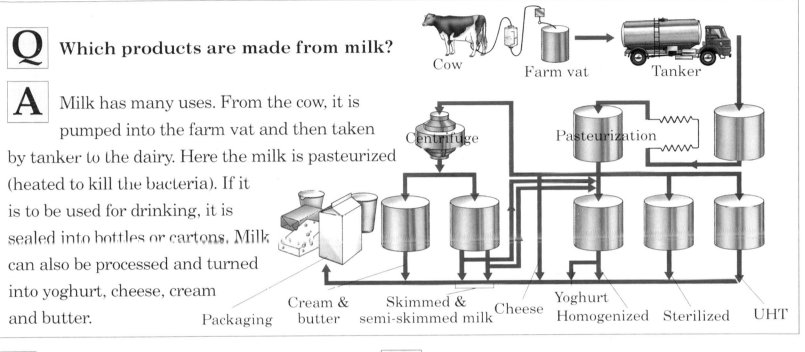

Cow Farm vat Tanker

Centrifuge Pasteurization

Packaging Cream & butter Skimmed & semi-skimmed milk Cheese Yoghurt Homogenized Sterilized UHT

Q Which fruits grow in tropical areas?

A Tropical regions are hot all the year round. Here are some of the fruits which grow in these areas.

1. Pineapple, 2. Durian, 3. Carambola, 4. Mango, 5. Pawpaw, 6. Soursop, 7. Persimmon, 8. Mangosteen, 9. Pomegranate, 10. Litchi, 11. Akee, 12. Cherimoya, 13. Banana, 14. Guava, 15. Sapodilla, 16. Passion fruit, 17.Loquat, 18.Cape gooseberry, 19.Rambutan.

Q Which countries have the most sheep?

A Australia is the biggest producer of sheep and wool in the world. In fact the country contains more sheep (about 138 million) than humans (just 17 million). New Zealand is another major sheep producer with some 74 million sheep. The human population is only 3.5 million, so that's about 20 sheep for every person! Many sheep are raised on the flat grasslands of South Africa, Argentina and Uruguay, as well as in China and India.

SCIENCE & TECHNOLOGY

INDEX

INDEX